Register of the Rev. John Macmillan: Being a Record of Marriages and Baptisms Solemnised by Him Among the Cameronian Societies

John Mackmillan

REGISTER

OF THE

REV. JOHN MACMILLAN

Being a Record of Marriages and Baptisms
solemnised by him among the
Cameronian Societies

EDITED BY

REV. HENRY PATON, M.A.,

EDINBURGH

Edinburgh

PRINTED BY LORIMER & CHALMERS, 31 ST. ANDREW SQUARE

1908

PREFACE

A SMALL paper book, about seven and a-half inches long by six inches broad, and scarcely an inch thick, bound in limp vellum, with vellum strings to tie and keep it shut, of the size to be easily placed in one's pocket and carried about, lies in the General Register House at Edinburgh. It is the record of the marriages and baptisms of the Covenanter men and women and their children during the period of the ministrations of the Rev. John Macmillan to the scattered companies or praying Societies between the years 1706 and 1751. When Dr. Matthews, the Secretary of the Pan-Presbyterian Alliance, addressed the Scottish Synod at its meeting in 1906, he mentioned that he had seen this book, and suggested that some means should be taken at least to secure its contents for the Church, and as the result of negotiations, Sir Stair Agnew, the Registrar-General for Scotland, has given permission for this to be done.

The little book seems to have belonged to William Galloway, a merchant in Glasgow, who, in the later years of his life, removed to Elie in Fife, and died there in 1853 or 1854. At the sale of his effects which followed, the book was purchased by the Rev. Walter Wood of that town, and may have been by him handed to Mr. George Robertson of the Register House, who deposited it for safe keeping among the public records of baptisms, marriages, and deaths therein preserved. And if these are justly valued by the nation for the information they afford, to Covenanters this little book, as the only authentic record of that kind relating to them, is surely of equal value, yea more; for some, finding the

S. H. Fields 27 Dec 1906 (in the index)

family from which their own descent is traceable, will feel the thrill of gratitude when therein they realise the unfailing truth of the Divine promise—

> " And to their children's children still
> His righteousness extends :
> To such as keep His covenant,
> And mindful are alway
> Of His most just commandements,
> That they may them obey."

The opening paragraph of the book discloses the intention of at first making it a Session Minute Book, but obviously this was impossible in an itinerant ministry, and so it at once resolves itself into a register. There are one or two cases of discipline recorded. It will be noticed that many of the baptisms are of grown-up boys and girls, the ordinance having been waited for in faith until it could be conscientiously obtained. The book adds much to our knowledge of Mr. Macmillan's laborious services to the Church, and it has a special interest in having come to light at the bi-centenary (1906) of his uptaking of that work.

It has been thought good to reprint the Register without modernising the spelling or phraseology, these possessing a quaintness and a flavour which will be pleasing to all interested readers.

REGISTER

OF THE

REV. JOHN MACMILLAN;

Being a Record of Marriages and Baptisms solemnised by him among the Cameronian Societies.

THERE being nothing left in record (so far as is yet known) by the godly and faithfull ministers in the late suffering times, [such] as Messrs. D. C.; R. C.; J. R.; D. H.* and that throwgh the perilous[ness] of the times, being hunted from place to place without any ce[rtain] abode, so that tho they practically observed the method of the C[hurch] of Scotland as far as their circumstances then could allow as to church discipline, yet there being no church register ex[tant?] of their procedings, and the times now not being as yet so turbulent, the minister and elders have thought fitt to set doun the methode in which they proceed with reference to their debarring and admitting to church priviledges, quherin they highly respect and imitate the comely order of the Church of Scotland as far as their circumstantiate case will alow them, and also desires to imitate the well-knoŭn practise of these our worthy ministers as abovsaid.

Its ordained that there be a Session Book, and all things pertaining to a Session be therin insert.

And first, as to Baptisms, its ordained that all the children who are baptized that their names be insert in the said Session Book together with the day, place, and their age, and the parents to whom they belong, and the parish quher they live.

2do. According to the comely order quhen both parents are in felloŭschip and no just exceptions against the father, that he present his oŭn child.

3io. That quher on of the parents is but in felloŭship (if upon examinatione they be found qualified) that that person take on the tyes.

4to. It is thought fitt that tho both the parents be of one judgment as to the testimony, that if for some fault or other they be laid aside, the elder or elders of the bounds is to acquant the

* That is, Donald Cargill, Richard Cameron, James Renwick, and probably David Houston.

I

minister of the grounds for quhich they were cast out, and this before they have the priviledge of baptizme, who is to deall with them as he and the elders sees expedient.

5to. Its to be observed that quher neither of the parents hes been in felloŭship and yet desirous of baptizm to their child or children, that as its judged necessary that all have testymonialls, both they within felloŭship and they without it, so that the elders nixt to them be at all due pains to inquire into the circumstances of such, and how they stand in judgment and practise as to the present testymony, and accordingly they are to be dealt with.

2do. With reference to Church censures, as to these that are guilty of fornicatione and other things relative to a Session, we judge that as they are to observe the usswall dyets for their publick apearances according to the Acts of the Generall Assemblys in the best times, so also we judge fitt that these publick appearences be as near the place quher the fact was comitted as circumstances will allow; and also in case that if any of our number should be scanalized, that their purgatione be as near that place or parish where they are slandered as posible can be.

3io. As to Mariadg (1mo.) we judge it expediant that the parties to be proclamed not only that they have their parents consent and aloŭance of the thing (as is set doun in the Directorey for Worship), but likewise that they have sufficient testymonialls from the felloŭship to whom they belong or from the best respected and honest about them if it cannot be had from the felloŭship, and if there be any thing found thats scandalus either of these within fellowship or without, that the minister have notice thereof before they go on to proclamatione. (2do.) Its judged that according to Church order the usswall times of proclamatione be observed, and that as far as our circumstances can allow us, and that as near the bounds as posible.

(4to.) As to the collections for the poor, we judge it fitt that a list of the names of the poor belonging to us be taken up and set doun in the Session Book. (2do.) That the day and place quher the collections were gathered be also sett doun, together with the quoto. (3to.) That these throw the severall shyres be brought to the Generall Meeting and destribut then as minister and elders sees fitt.

Children baptized at Craford John, December second day, 1706.
    The children of Dunkan Forbes in Borroŭstouness : —Katrine, aged 13 years.
    Of James Carmichaell in the paroch of Carmichaell : —Daniell, aged 12 ; Isobell, aged 10 ; William, aged 8.
    Of Margaret Anderson in the paroch of Moorkirk : —Christin, aged 15 ; Mary, aged 10.
    Of Tho[mas] Caderheed in the paroch of Shots : —John, aged 1.

Of Mathew Flager in the paroch of Cragie :—John, aged 14.

Of Grisell Johnstoun in the paroch of Crafoord, December 3, at tüo in the morning :—James, aged 1.

1706, December 23, Morisons haven, children of Alexander Hariots :—Christin, aged 15, 3 quarters ;   , aged 13 ;   , aged 10, 6 months.

Of William Haals, in Stobs :—   , aged 13 ;   , aged 9 ;   , aged 3.

Fyfe. December 26, in Kinnocher paroch, the children of William Nicolson :—Elizabeth, aged 14 ; Marey, aged 12 ; James, aged 8 ; Ann, aged 8 ; Janet, aged 4.

Eodem die, in St. Andrews, David Mathison children :—Jean, aged 15 ; Andrew, aged 12 ; Christin, aged 9 ;   , aged 7 ;   , aged 4 ;   , aged 2.

Ede[nburgh], 30 December, Johns Tunnos child,   , aged   .

At Suyn Know in the paroch of New Munkland, Janwary fyft day, 1707.—

William Robison in the paroch of Bothwell, children :— Rebekah, aged 6 ; William, aged 5.

James Hamilton in the toun of Hamiltoun :—James, aged 3 ; Elizabath, aged 5 moneths.

John Ingles in the paroch of Shots :—Marion, aged 8 ; John, aged 5.

Thomas Ingles in the paroch of Shots :—Helen, aged 4 ; David, aged 2.

John Russell in the paroch of Shotts :—John, aged 2 ; Janet, aged 7 moneths.

Samuell Young in the paroch of Torphichan :—David, aged 2 ; Agnes, aged 11 weeks.

John Nimmo in the paroch of Shots :—Janet, aged 3.

Alexander Garner in the paroch of Shotts :—Agnes, aged 4 ; William, aged 2.

William Allan in the paroch of New Munkland :—John, aged 4 ; William, aged 6 moneths.

Thomas Newlands in the paroch of Shotts :—Jean, aged 15 ; Janet, aged 12 ; Elspith, aged 5.

David Young in the paroch of New Munkland :—David, aged 10 ; Samuel, aged 8 ; Lillias, aged 5 ; Agnes, aged 2.

Thomas Main in the paroch of New Munkland :—Charels, aged 4 ; Agnes, aged 1.

John Hill in the paroch of New Munkland :—John, aged 4 ; Andrew, aged 15 dayes.

John Miller in the paroch of New Munkland :—James, aged 4 ; John, aged 2.

John Russell in the paroch of Shotts (Thomas Newlands,

sponsor, the parent grosly ignorant) :—Samuell, aged 4 ; Petter, aged 2.

George Jackson in the Barony of Glasgow :—Janet, aged 16 and 6 months.

David Selkirk in the paroch of West Munkland :—William, aged 3 quarters.

James Selchrig in the paroch of West Munkland :—Elspith, aged 2.

Robert Wark in the paroch of Calder :—James, aged 2.

John Jackson in the toun of Glasgow :—George, aged 7.

John Martine in the paroch of Carnwath :—John, aged 6 months.

John Ingles in the paroch of Carmichaell :—Robert, aged 10.

John Cuthell in the paroch of Logie, Stirlingshyre :—John, aged 1.

James Hamilton in the paroch of Bothwell (James Smelie, sponsor, the parent under scandall not absolved) :— Margaret, aged 6.

Margaret Urrie in the paroch of Kilbryde :—Marion, aged 15 ; William, aged 13.

Andrew Aull in the paroch of New Munkland :—John, aged 3.

James Crafoord in the paroch of New Munkland :—Charels, aged 4 ; Agnes, aged 1.

John Patterson in the parish of Kinkaren :—Mary, aged 7 ; Janet, aged 4 ; Isobell, aged 2.

Margaret Edmistoun in the parish of Kilmadock :—John, aged 7.

At Carphin Byars in the paroch of Bothwell, Janwary 6 day, 1707.—

William Robison in the paroch of Bothwell :—Bethea, aged 3 ; James, aged 5 quarters.

Margaret Scot in the paroch of Bothwell :—John, aged 2 ; Robert, aged 1.

John Gillies in the paroch of Dalyell :—Bethea, aged 9 ; Margaret, aged 6 ; Christin, aged 1.

James Smith in the paroch of Bothwell :—William, aged 8 ; James, aged 5 ; Alexander, aged 4 ; Robert, aged 3.

Robert Fullertoun in the paroch of Dalserf :—Margaret, aged 6 ; Robert, aged 2 ; Jean, aged 15 dayes.

At Castell Hill of Tinwald in Nith, Janwary 12, 1707.—

Margaret Watson in the paroch of Closeburn, ansuered for herself, her parents being dead, aged 15.

Jean Ferguson, aged 7 ; Isobell Wattson sponsor, in the paroch of Closeburn.

John Mundell in the paroch of Torthorwald :—Janet, aged 12 ; Robert, aged 10 ; John, aged 8 ; William, aged 2.

Luke Frizell in the paroch of Closeburn :—Elspith, aged 10 ;

Samuell Young in paroch of Torphighan :—James, aged a
moneth.

David Selchrig in Old Munkland :—James, aged 4 moneths.

Thomas Inglies in paroch of Shots :—Robert, aged 14 weeks.

Eskdale, December 5 and 6, 1709—baptised 27.

Forrest, December 8—baptised 4.

Tivot, December 15—3.

East Loth[ian], December 23—6.

Fyf, December 26—11.

Edenburgh, December 30—1.

October 22, 1709.—

George Young in the parish of Finick :—Mathew, aged an
year old.

Adam Gaw in the parish of Douglas :—May 7, 1710,
William, aged 8 dayes.

Ja. Pet in the parish of Douglas :—Janet, aged a moneth.

William Willson in parish of Carmichall :—Jo., aged 3 quarters.

Jo. Williamson in parish of Carmichaell :—Thomas, aged
half a year.

Glencarn, February 24, 1710.—

Jo. Gibsons child, Isobell, aged a moneth.

Jo. Carsans child, Rob, aged a moneth.

At Pentland, May 2, 1710.—

James Umpherston, his son and daughter, James and Helen
Umpherston, twins, born April 16, 1710, wer baptized
by the Rev. Mr. Jo. M'Millan.

At the Bayers in parish of Bothwell, March 2nd, 1710,
baptised four.—

Moffet hills in parish of Shots, March 6, 1710.—

David Young in New Munkland :—Ann, aged 19 weeks.

Tho. Main in parish of Shots :—Patrick, aged 10 weeks.

William Martin in parish of Shots :—Agnas, aged 20 dayes.

Jo. Martin in paroch of Carnwath :—   aged   .

Jo. Wilson in paroch of Carnwath :—   aged   .

Jo. Selchrig in Old Munkland :—Margret, aged 10 weeks.

Tho. Caderhead in parish of Shots :—Thomas, aged 20
weeks.

Alexander Garner in parish of Old Munkland :—John, aged
half an year.

William Dick in paroch of Airth :—William, aged 24 weeks.

Craford John, May 1, 1709.—

Alexander Weir, the forsaid parish :—Mary, aged an quarter.

May 2nd, 1709.—

Hugh Muir in parish of Douglas:—Margret, aged 6 moneths.

Caraford John, July 16, 1710.—

Mathew Neuland in parish of Shots:—Elspith, aged 10 weeks.

July 17, 1710.—

Thomas Wood in parish of Crafoord:—Thomas, aged 32
weeks.

At Kersland milln in Dalry, November 8, 1710.—
  Hector Thomson in Kilmawers had a daughter baptised
    called Jean, born the 12 of September, 1710.
December 1, 1711.—
  Alexander Borland in the parish of Evandale, a son called
    John, born July 18th, 1710.
  James Muir in Evandale, a son called James, aged 18 weeks
    3 days.
  John Mickle had a child baptiz'd the same time.
March 10th, 1711.—
  James Donaldson in parish of Eskdalemuir had a daughter
    baptized called Mary.
March 11.—
  Robert Johnstoun in Applegirth a daughter named Elizabeth.
  Matthew Short in the parish of Moffat a son named John.
At Henshelwood, November ult., 1711.—
  To James Paterson in the parish of Carstairs, a son called
    George.
  To John Davie there, a daughter Isobel.
  To Thomas Barry there, a son called Thomas.
At Johnstoun, December ult., 1711.—
  To John Watson, the parish of Greenock, a son called John,
    born September ult., 1711.—
  To Alexander Porter in Greenock, a daughter named
    Margaret.
Aprile 29, 1710, at Castlehill.—
  To Gavin Lawrie in the parish of Carluke, a son James,
    10 weeks old.
  To Matthew Newlands in Livingston, Elizabeth, May 8, 1710.
Feb. . . ., 1710.—
  To Richard Dobie in the parish of Carluke, a son Thomas,
    aged 3 months.
At Henshelwood, November 3, 1710.—
  To James Clarkson in the parish of Carnwath, a daughter
    Margaret.
  To John Wilson there, a son Alexander.
  To John Martin there, a daughter Mary.
At Irongath Braes, March 19th, 1710.—
  To Robert Forbes in Bathgate, a son named Robert, born
    December 3rd, 1709.
Moorkirk, May 26, 1712.—
  John Murdoch, a daughter named Margaret, 10 weeks old.
  John Ranken in Moorkirk, a daughter named Jean, 6 weeks old.
  Archibald Gai in Moorkirk, a daughter Helene, 7 days old.
In Egleham at Trees, November 25, 1712.—
  To Alexander Porter in Greenock parish, a daughter called
    Elizabeth, 11 months old.
  To Andrew Watson, indweller in Glasgow, a son named
    Andrew, 13 months old.

At Henshelwood, May 12, 1712.—

To Thomas Barry in Carstairs, a son called James.

To John Davie there, a son called James.

To John White there, a daughter called Jonet.

At . . ., 1712.—

To John Welsh, two sons called James and Joseph, one 8 years and the other 6.

To William Yule in Crawfordmoor, a son John; *item*, another son James, baptiz'd October, 1712.

John Blacklaw in Campshead had a child baptiz'd at the same time, called Catharine.

At Keppoch in Baronny of Glasgow, 2nd Sabbath of February, 1713.—

To Robert Galloway in the parish of Lenzie, a son called James, 9 weeks old.

To William Dobie in Easter Linzie, a daughter Agnes, 8 month old.

To Michael Thomson in parish of New Monkland, a daughter, Agnes, 8 months old.

To John Murhead in Dalzeel parish, a son called James, 15 weeks old.

To William Summers in Baronny of Glasgow, a son William, 10 weeks old.

To William Watson in Rutherglen parish, a daughter called Betthea, 20 weeks old.

To John Cunnigham in the parish of Shots, a son called William, 11 weeks old.

Crawfordjohn, May 25, 1713.—

To David Moffat in Crawfordmoor, a daughter Margaret, half a year old.

To Robert Kennedy in the parish of Douglas, a son Andrew, 6 weeks old.

May 24th, 1713.—

Baptized to John Black in Finglen in Eskdalemoor a son named Adam.

To James Moffat in Glengeith in parish of Crawfordmoor a son named Thomas.

At Borrowstounness, January 11, 1713.—

To John M'Vey in Borrowstouness a son called William, born December 2nd, 1712.

To John Chrystie in Slamanen parish a son named Thomas, born 22nd August, 1712, and baptized January 20, 1713.

To William Shaw in Bathgate a daughter called Jonet, born July 10, 1712, baptized there January 21, 1713.

To William Martin in Shots a daughter called Jean, born 2nd August, 1712.

To Thomas Miller in Morronside a son called John.

October . . ., 1712, At Crawfordjohn.—
James Moffat in Glengeith a daughter Mary.
John Douglass in the parish of Robertoun had a daughter named Catharine.
To Matthew Newlands in Tarphichen parish a son called John, born December 27, 1711, baptized at Cloakburn July 26, 1712.
At Haughead, October 6, 1712.—
To Andrew Waddie a daughter called Mary.
At Craigmui, October   , 1709.—
To James Harkness in Juxta, two children brought out of Ireland, Robert, aged 10 years, and Mary, aged 4 years.
At Pentland, August 4, 1708.—
Mr. John M'Neil and Beatrix Umpherston were married by the Rev. Mr. John M'Millan. Their son, William M'Neil, born September 9th, 1711, was baptized by Mr. John M'Millan at Pentland, September 12, 1711.
At Ramstone, November 9, 1710.—
Joseph Francis in Irvine :—Joseph, 11 weeks old.
Hector Thomson in Kilmawers :—Jean, 8 weeks old.
At Johnstoun in Clydsdale, December 30, 1711.—
William Stirling in Old Monkland :—Jean, 9 days old.
Margaret Callendar in Old Monkland :—Robert, 3 quarters of year, and eight days old.
James Mitchel in Old Calder :—John, 26 weeks old.
Robert Urie in Govan :—Jean, 3 quarters old.
John Watson in Greenock :—John, 13 weeks old.
John Wardrope in Eastwood :—Walter, 12 months old.
Patrick Love in Kilmalcomb :—William, 7 months old.
James Laird . . . :—Alexander, 12 months old.
Margaret Urie in Rutherglen :—James Tindal, 3 quarters old.
Jonet Craig in Paisley :—Jean Cleeland, 5 quarters old.
At Water of Endrick, February 15, 1713.—
Thomas Edmond in Killearn :—Joseph, born about the middle of January, 1712.
James M'Gilchrist in Kippen :—Jean, aged about a year.
At Logie, November 26, 1712.—
James Allein in Dennie, a daughter Jonet, 14 years old.
William Thomson in Stirling :—William, four months old.
George Farrier in Stirling :—James, 7 months old.
At Tinwald, January 8, 1710.—
To James Wilkin in Closeburn, a daughter named Margaret.
To Edward Beck in Tinwald, a daughter named Jean.
At Burn of Tinwald, January 9, 1710.—
To Thomas Gillespy in Closeburn, a son called George.
At Kilburn, January 16, 1710.—
To David Jarden in Applegirth a son named John.

January 12, 1710.—
> To George Henderson in Hoddam a son called James, born October, 1708.
> To Christopher Calvert a daughter called Jean.

Att Marjory Muir, January 29, 1711.—
> To John Crichtoun in the parish of Glencairn, a daughter Kathrine.
> To John Watson in the parish of Closeburn, a daughter Jonet.
> To Archbald Glencorss in Closeburn a daughter called Mary.
> To James Mattheson in Closeburn a son named Robert. All these in the first year of their age.

At Birkhill, January 30, 1711.—
> Robert Douglas in Closeburn had a daughter baptizd called Agnes, born January 15, 1711.
> John Edgar in Tinwald had a daughter baptiz'd called Jean, born October 28, 1709.
> William Black in Tinwald had a son baptiz'd John, aged one year.
> James Cowan in Kirkmahoe had a daughter baptiz'd Jean, born September 25, 1710.
> Luke Frissel in Kirkmahoe, a daughter baptiz'd Mary.
> Katharine Mundel had a son baptiz'd named James Carruthers, supposed son to James Caruthers, chyrurgeon ; Herbert Wales, sponsor.

January 5, 1711.—
> Robert Mundel in Tinwald had a daughter baptiz'd Rebecca, aged 7 months.

February 1, 1711, At Eglefechen.—
> William Mattheson in Middlebie had a daughter baptiz'd called Jonet.
> Archbald Grieve in the parish of Lochmaben had a son baptiz'd Robert.

February , 1711.—
> George Henderson in Hoddam had a daughter named Jonet, born December 1, 1710.

At Coldoons, August 12, 1711.—
> John Stevenson in Hoddam had a son named John.

At Tinwald, Aprile 27, 1712.—
> James M'Kun in Keir had a son baptiz'd named Alexander, and a daughter named Sarah.
> James Paterson in the parish of Tinron had a daughter named Margaret.
> William M'Vittie in the parish of Kirkmichael had a son baptiz'd James.
> John Frizzel in Tinwald had a daughter named Rebecca, aged one year.
> Edward Beck in Tinwald had a daughter named Jonet.

Aprile 28, 1712.—

Luke Frizzel, younger, in Tinwald, had a daughter named Jonet, born April 17th.

Alexander Dove in Kirkmahoe had a son baptiz'd named John, born October 15, 1711.

John Edgar, younger, had a son called Thomas, aged two years ; John Edgar, elder, being sponsor.

At Coldoons, May 4, 1712.—

Andrew Wells in Kirkpatrick-juxta, had a son named Joseph, a quarter old.

David Jerdan in Applegirth had a son named David, 18 weeks old.

James Knox in Cummertrees had a son baptiz'd David, aged half a year.

John Roddick in Cummertrees had a daughter baptiz'd Helen, aged one month.

At Tinwald, August 10, 1712.—

Archbald Grieve in Lochmaben had a son named Thomas, aged 11 weeks.

William M'Vittie in Garrel had a daughter baptized named Jonet, aged 3 weeks.

James Wilkin in Closeburn, a son aged six months called John.

At Barnmoor in Closeburn, August 11, 1712.—

John Watson in Closeburn had a daughter called Hellen, 7 days old.

James Mattheson in Closeburn had a daughter called Grizzel, aged 5 months and one week.

At Coldoons, August 17, 1712.—

John Forsyth in Hoddam, a son called Jacob, aged one month.

James M'Vittie in Garrald had a son called James, aged half a year.

John Mundel in Torthorald had a daughter called Mary.

At Glencrosh in Glencairn, April 19, 1713.—

Thomas Grierson in Kells had a daughter named Margaret, aged a year and threequarters.

Samuel Clark in Dalmelintoun had a son called James, aged a year and half.

Thomas M'Adam in Glencairn had a son named James, born August 17, 1712.

At Nackleshang in Closeburn, Aprile 23, 1713.—

Robert Douglas had a son called Samuel, born December 11, 1712.

Thomas Gillespy in Closeburn :—Isobel, aged half a year and six weeks.

At Nuchleshang, Aprile 26, 1713.—

David Moffat in Crawford :—Margaret, aged 6 weeks.

James Harkness in Juxta :—James, aged 9 weeks.

Samuel Stuart in Tarregles :—Elizabeth, born November 30, 1712.

Matthew Short in Moffat :—Agnes, four months old.

William Spence . . . :—Jean, aged 15 years.

John Hope in Juxta :—Margaret, a quarter old.

Alexander Wilson in Johnstoun :—Matthew, born February 17, 1713.

John Frizzel in Kirkmichael :—Jean, one month.

At Hartbush, Aprile 28, 1713.—

William Duthie in Torthorald :—Mary, born March 8, 1711.

John Robison in Tinwald :—Jonet, born August 17, 1712.

At Coldoons, May 3, 1713.—

George Henderson in Hoddam :—Giles, born Aprile 11, 1713.

William Black in Middlebee :—Ann, a quarter old.

William Matheson in Middlebee :—Bethea, January 7, 1713.

At Birkhill, March 13, 1715.—

Adam Johnston in Moffat :—Agnes, 7 weeks old.

Ibid. ; March 14, 1715.—

William Wales, Hoddam :—John, born 21, 1714. (*sic.*)

John Frizzel in Tinald :—Michael, born March 17, 1714.

Robert Barton in Tinwald :—James, born June 17, 1714.

Edward Beck in Tinwald :—Jean, born July ult., 1714.

Robert Douglas in Closeburn :—William, aged a month.

John Watson in Closeburn :—John, aged . . . .

Archibald Glencors, Closeburn :—Jonet, aged a quarter of a year.

Andrew Glover in Tinwald :—Jonet, aged 7 months.

Luke Frizzel in Kirkmahoe :—William, born April 27, 1714.

Thomas Wightman in Kirkmahoe :—Grissel.

James Patoun in Closeburn :—Mary, born 23rd August, 1714.

Thomas M'Vittie in Kirkmichael :—John.

Alexander Wilson in Johnstoun :—Thomas.

March 22, 1716, at Hartbush.—

John Edgar in Kirkmahoe :—Jonet, born March 27, 1715; his father, John Edgar, being sponsor.

William Swan in Kirkmahoe :—Jonet, 3 quarters of year old.

William Wales in Tinwald :—Jonet, born November 25, 1716. (*sic.*)

Thomas Edgar in Tinwald :—Sarah, born July 5, 1715.

William M'Vittie in Johnston :—William, aged a quarter of year.

At Hartbush, April 1, 1716.—

Edward Hastie in Johnstoun :—Jonet, born a week before Hallowday.

At Todhill in Clydsdale, July 3rd, 1715.—

Alexander Smith in the parish of Bothwel :—Marion, a quarter old.

James Hamilton in parish of Bothwel :—James, born October 16, 1714.

William Scot in Old Monkland :—Isobel, nineteen weeks old.

Gavin Bogle, Old Monkland :—John, born 1 of April, 1714.

William Findlay in Old Monkland :—John, October 2, 1714.

Adam Selkirk, Old Monkland :—Jonet, born January 11, 1715.

John Watson in Greenock :—Agnes, born October 10, 1714.

Andrew Watson in Glasgow :—Elizabeth.

James Burns in Hamiltoun :—Margaret, born June 28, 1715.

William Allein in Monkland :—Joseph, half a year old.

Arthur Gardner in Old Monkland :—Grissel, born October 15, 1715, Hugh Miller being sponsor.

John Miller in Shots :—John, born March 31, 1714.

At Cambuslang, February 25, 1713.—

James Burns in Hamiltoun :—James, 13 days old.

At Drumclog, February 24.—

Hector Thomson in Kilmawers :—Mary, born June 28, 1712.

Joseph Francis in Irvine :—Mary, born September 2, 1712.

James Morison in Evandale :—John, eighteen weeks old.

At Crawfordjohn, May 10, 1716.—

Robert Kennedy in Douglas :—William, about a quarter old.

Archbald Gay in Moorkirk :—William, 16 weeks old.

Alexander Williamson in Crawford :—Mary, 3 quarters old.

Alexander Weir in Crawfordjohn :—John, a quarter old.

At Caldercrooks, June 13, 1716.—

John Newlands in Shots :—Janet, 5 quarters old.

James Bennet in Carnwath :—Margare, 12 weeks old.

Thomas Greenshiels in Carnwath :—Elizabeth.

James Russel in Shots :—John, 12 weeks old.

James Nilson in Shots :—Gavin, 12 weeks old.

William Pillans in Shots :—William, 24 weeks old.

Thomas Fairly in Livingstoun :—Thomas, 22 weeks old.

Jonet Edgar in Shots :—Robert, 13 months old.

John Wilson in Carnwath :—Jonet, 18 days old.

William Whitlay in Shots :—Elizabeth, 6 months old.

John Mann in Carnwath :—Walter, 6 months old.

Alexander Walker in Shots :—Jonet, 31 weeks old.

Blair Muiks, August 2, 1715.—

John Christie in Torphichen :—Agnes, born July 10, 1714.

William Burd in Bathgate :—Jonet, born April 14, 1714.

John Davie in Carstairs :—Marion, 6 months old.

James Bennet, Carnwath :—Robert, born January *ult.*, 1714.

Persons married by Mr. John M‘Millan, minister of the Gospel, within the Correspondence of Midlothian and Twadel, viz. :—

Munday, the 12th of November, 1711, marryed at Pentland, Mr. Jo. M‘Mains and Anne Floyd in Edinburgh. *Ditto*, James Gifford and Margaret Penman. The tenth of Aprile

1712, marryed at Crawfoordjohn, Mr. Charles Umpherston and Elizabeth Bailie in Pentland. Munday the 7th of September, 1713. Marryed in Edinburgh, James Currie and Agnes Burn in Tweedale.

Children baptized *ibidem*, Two to Mr. Jo. M'Neil, preacher. Thomas, son to David Donaldson, glover in Edinburgh, May 1712. James Umpherston had some baptized. Helene, daughter to Mr. Charles Umpherston in Pentland. Alexander, son to Alexander Tenent, shoemaker in Calton at Edinburgh. James Gifford at Currie had a child baptiz'd. Janet, daughter to James Brigton, baptized at the Boarstone, 1712.

At Keppoch, February 22, 1713. Baptized to—
James Mitchel in Calder parish, a son James, 5 weeks old.
David Selkirk in Old Monkland, a son John, one day old.
Hugh Miller *ibid.*, a son called Andrew, a year old.
Thomas Hill in Glasgow Laigh Kirk, a daughter Christian, 12 weeks old.
Andrew Burnside in Glasgow *ibid.*, a daughter Agnes, 20 weeks old.
William Mitchel in Barrony parish, a son John, born September 15, 1712.
John Tod in Barony parish, a son Robert, four years old.
James Brownlee in Easter Linzie, a daughter Jonet, born July 1, 1712.
Andrew Menzies in Barrony parish, a son Andrew, 11 weeks old.
James Stuart in Govan, a daughter Elizabeth, born January 3, 1713.
Robert Urie in Govan, a son Robert, born November 7, 1712.
At Bancrief Hills, September 20th, 1713. Baptized to—
David Newlands in Shotts, a son David, born June 24, 1713.
William Dick in Airth, a daughter Jean, born July 14, 1713.
John Pearson in Borrowstouness, Jean, born June 16, 1713.
William Russell of Arus in Cumbernald, a son John, born September 5, 1713.
John Wark in . . ., a daughter Katherine, born August 2, 1713.
To James Clerkson in Carnwath, a son Alexander, born July 14, 1713.
At Badshaw, September 27, 1713. Baptized to—
Robert Eaton in Bothwel, a son Robert, two years old.
John Goodwin in Barrony, a son Allan, four-and-twenty hours old.
John Miller in Bothwel, a daughter Jean, born March 6, 1713.
William Scot in old Monkland, a daughter Margaret, 19 weeks old.

2

Thomas Watson in Stenhouse, a son Thomas, 8 weeks old.

Gavin Laurie in Carluke, a daughter Margaret, 14 weeks old.

Alexander Burn in Dalserf, a daughter Jonet, 10 weeks old.

At Pollock, October 3d, 1713.   Baptized to—

Archbald Wright in Aranthrow, a daughter Isobel, aged 5 weeks.

John Lang in Lissen, a daughter Mary, born May 20th, 1700.

James Laird in Kilmalcomb, a daughter Margaret, half-a-year old.

William Steven in Glasgow, a son John, born June 12, 1713.

Alexander Young in Eglesham, a son James, born April 1, 1713.

John Wilson in Eglesham, a son John, born November 19, 1712.

Archbald Thomson in Barronry, a daughter Isobel, born February 7, 1713.

At Crawfords Dyke, October 7th, 1713.   Baptized to —

John Watson in Crawfoords Dyke, a son William, 8 weeks old.

Agnes Galbraith in Kilmacolm, a daughter Mary, aged half a year and 7 weeks.

Alexander Portar in Greenock, a daughter Mary, born March 21, 1713.

At Gaalstoun, October 15, 1713.   Baptized to—

Alexander Boreland in Evandale, a son Alexander, born May 15, 1713.

James Train in Evandale, a son Henry, born March 6, 1713.

Matthew Nisbet in Lowdon, a son Hugh, born May 6, 1713.

At Crawfoordjohn, February 28, 1714.   Baptized to—

John Williamson in Crawfoordmoor, a daughter Margaret, 3 quarters old.

James Brigtoun in Crawfoordjohn, a son James.

William Thomson in Crawfoordmoor, a daughter Jonet, 4 months old.

James Forsyth in Durisdier, a son John, one month old.

James Thomson in Crawfoordmoor, a daughter Margaret, born February 15, 1714.

At Crawfoordjohn, May 30, 1714.   Baptized to—

Robert Young in Leshmahago, a daughter Jonet, 11 weeks old.

William Yuil in Crawfoordmoor, a son Adam, 3 weeks old.

George Kilpatrick in Leshmahego, a son Daniel, aged 6 weeks.

James Pate in Dowglas, a son Robert, aged 3 months.

John Steinson in Lishmahego, a daughter Mary, 22 dayes old.

Thomas Carmichall in Crawfordjohn, a daughter Agnes, a month old.

Adam French in Crawfoordmoor, a daughter Bessie, a year and five weeks old.

At Caldercrooks, July 23, 1714. Baptized to—
John Burn in Bothwell, a daughter Bethea, 10 days old.
William Kirkwood in Bothwel, a daughter Margaret, 14 days
old.
Robert Thomson in Dalserf, Margaret, born the last
Wednesday of February, 1714.
At Bathgate, August 22, 1714. Baptized to—
James Dunlop in East Calder, a son James, born the last of
February 1714.
At Borrowstounness, August 17, 1714. Baptized to—
Alexander Mattheson in Carridden, a daughter called Marion,
born Aprile 12, 1714.
At Loanhead.—
Mr. John M'Neil his son James, born March 12, 1713, was
baptized by the Rev. Mr. John M'Millan.
At Biggar, May 23, 1712.—
James Umpherston in Pentland his daughter Elizabeth, born
February 29, 1712, was baptized by the Rev. Mr. John
M'Millan.
At Crawfordjohn, April 16, 1716. Baptized to—
Adam Gaa in Dowglass, a son Adam, born December 17,
1715.
William Moffat in Twadsmoor parish, a son called James,
born March 14, 1716.
Robert Govan in Crawfoordjohn, a son John, born November
15, 1715.
James Jack in Govan, a daughter Agnes, aged 20 weeks.
At Crawfoordjohn, August 2d, 1716. Baptized to—
John Cuthbertson in Walston, a daughter Agnes, born the
27 of May, 1716.
Robert Young in Lishmahego, a son Robert, 11 weeks
old.
At Loanhead, were baptized after lecture by the Rev. Mr. John
M'Millan :—
Helen M'Neil, daughter to Mr. John M'Neil, born February
5, 1715.
Isobel Hasty, daughter to James Hasty in Lasswade parish,
born November 7, 1714.
At Crawfoordjohn, May 12, 1717. Baptized to—
Robert Kennedy in Dowglass, a son William, about a
quarter old.
Archibald Gai in Moorkirk, William, 16 weeks old.
Alexander Williamson in Crawford, 3 quarters old.
Alexander Weir in Crawfoordjohn, a son called John, about
a quarter old.
At Pentland, August 24, 1714.—
James Umpherstone, his son Charles Umpherston, born
August 8, 1714, was baptized by the Rev. Mr. John
M'Millan.

At . . . ., June 13, 1713.—
James Giffard in Currie parish, his daughter Margaret, born May 27, 1713, was baptized by the Rev. Mr. John M'Millan.

At Barnmoor in the parish of Closeburn, February 17, 1717. Baptized to—
Robert Brown in parish of Keir :—Peter, born September 6, 1716.
Alexander Nivison in Closeburn :—John, born September 19, 1716.
James Cowan in parish of Kirk[m]aho :—Grizzel, born June 11, 1716.
James Summer in Closeburn :—James, born November 16, 1716.

At Caldercrooks, June 13, 1717. Baptized to—
Robert Galloway in parish of Calder, a son Robert, born May 25, 1717.
John Miller in the parish of Bothwel, a daughter Margaret, born January 1716.
James Hay in Cumbernald, a son John, born last of Aprile 1717.
Robert White in Morronside, a son John, born April 30, 1717.
Matthew Newlands in Bathgate, a son Thomas, born February 5, 1717.
William Russel in Shots, a son Robert, born cir[ca] August ult., 1716.
Richard Thomson in Shots, a daughter Mary, born 22d July.
William Paterson in Shots, a son James, born March 29, 1716.
John Walker in Shots, a daughter Margaret, November 1, 1716.
Thomas Miller in Cumbernald, a son James, born May 2, 1717.
Robert Paterson in Bothwel, a daughter Marion, born May 25, 1717.

At Loanhead.—
Mr. John M'Neil his daughter Janet, born October 24, 1717, was baptized by the Rev. Mr. John M'Millan.

At . . . .—
James Hasty and Isobel Forrest in Laswade parish, their daughter Katharine, born July 23, 1718, was baptized by Mr. John M'Millan.

At . . . ., February 27, 1717.—
James Giffard in Currie parish, his son James, born October 27, 1716, was baptized by the Rev. Mr. John M'Millan.

At Hartbush, March 24, 1718, was baptized to—
James M'Coon in parish of Keir, a daughter Mary, aged half a year.

Andrew Wells in Kirpatrickjuxta, a son James, aged half a year.

James Paterson in Closeburn, a son James, aged one year and an half.

Matthew Short in Moffat, a son Thomas.

Robert Johnston in Tinwald, a daughter Elspit, aged a quarter of year.

Andrew Glover in Tinwald, a daughter Susanna, aged 3 quarters of year.

John Edgar in Kirkmaho, a daughter Jean, born February 2d, 1718.

Edward Beck in Tinwald, a son John, aged one year and a half.

Thomas Edgar in Tinwald, a son John, born March 16, 1717.

John Walles in Tinwald, a daughter Jean.

At Wallacetoune in parish of Hoddam, March . . . , 1718, were baptized to—

John Carlyll in parish of Middleby, a son Thomas, born February 12, 1717.

William Patey in parish of . . . . , a daughter Jonet, born March 4, 1718.

William Black in parish of Middleby, a daughter Isobel, born March 14, 1717.

James Knox in . . . . , a daughter Margaret, born March 11, 1718.

Alexander Wilson in parish of Middleby, a son Alexander, born July 1717.

At Hartbush, October 14, 1718. Baptized to—

Thomas Brown in Closeburn, a son Thomas, aged about 6 months.

Edward Hastie in Johnston, a daughter Jean, born July 1, 1718.

At . . . . , baptized to—

James Findlay in the parish of Barrony, a son James.

James Witherspoon in Old Monkland, a daughter Isobel, born June 22, 1717.

George Leck in Calder parish, a son George, born August 27, 1717.

John Selkirk in Old Monkland, a son John, born July 10, 1718.

Alexander Walker in Calder parish, a son James, born July 19, 1718.

William Ralton in Calder parish, a son William, born 1 of July 1718.

David Selkirk in Barony parish, a daughter Lilias, 21 of Aprile 1718.

Thomas Wood in Monkland, a daughter Elizabeth, born August 1, 1717.

Gavin Black in Glasgow, a son Archbald, born May 29, 1718.

Andrew Menzies in Barrony parish, a son George, born November . . 1716.

William Summer in Glasgow, a daughter Jean, born July 31, 1718.

James Stirling in Old Monkland, a daughter Jonet, born March 19, 1718.

William Steven in Glasgow, a son Alexander born 29 August 1717.

At Caldercrooks, August 3d, 1718.   Baptized to—

John Thomson in Monkland, a son John.

William Easton in Shots, a daughter Agnes.

James Walker in Shots, a daughter Rachel.

Robert Dewart in Shots, a daughter Jonet.

Alexander Walker in Shots, a daughter Mary.

William Mason in Bothwel, a son Matthew.

James Clelland in Bothwell, a daughter Jean.

William Bruce in New Monkland, a daughter Jonet.

John Young in New Monkland, a son David.

James Russel in New Monkland, a son David.

John Steil in New Monkland, a son Thomas.

John Muirhead in Shots, a daughter Jonet, born March 18, John Inglis being sponsor for the child.

John Miller in Shots, a daughter Jean, born May 20, 1718.

Alexander Wright in Kilmackdock :—Alexander, born the 7 of April 1718.

John Galbraith in Balfroon :—Catharine, born last Sabbath of July 1718.

John Marshal in Old Monkland, a daughter Hellen.

George Russel in Shots, a daughter Elizabeth, born May 18, 1718.

Jonet Scot in Kilbride, a son Robert (Pirry), born June 9, 1717.

John Brown in Shots, a son David, born 2d 1717.

William Burd in Bathgate, a daughter Christiane, born September 1717.

William Scot in Westcalder, a son Walter, a quarter of year old.

Thomas Edmond in Kilearn, a daughter Elizabeth, born January 4, 1718.

John Christie in Tarphichen, a daughter Jonet, 25 of June 1717.

William Cadzin in Kilmackdock, a son William, born April 1, 1718.

James Nilson in Shots, a son James, born July 5, 1717.

John Davie in Carstares, a daughter Jonet, born August 8, 1717.

Robert Aiton in Mickle Govan, a son George, a year and 20 days old.

At Hartbush, July 19th, 1719. Baptized to—
Archbald Grieve in Dalton, a son Robert, aged 14 weeks.
Robert Barton in Tinwald, a son James, born January 25 instant.
William Wells in Hoddam, a daughter Agnes, aged 4 months.
Edward Beck in Tinwald, a son James, aged 7 months.
Robert Tait in Kirkmaho, a daughter Mary, born December 25, 1718.

At Crawfordjohn, August 3, 1719. Baptized to—
John M'Cloon in Durisdier, a daughter Agnes, born March 28, 1719.
John Vicars in Lishmahego, a daughter Isobel, born July 30, 1718.
John Paton in . . . ., a daughter Marion, born November 16, 1718.
John Paterson in Carstares, a son James, aged half a year.
John Burn in Lishmahego, a daughter Jonet, born March 14, 1719.
Adam French in Crawfoord Moor, a son John, born June 30, 1719.
Archbald Campbel in Dalzeel parish, aged 24 years.

At Drumclog, June 12, 1720. Baptized to—
Archbald Wright in Paisley, a daughter Mary, born October 27, 1719.
John Brown in Egglesham a son Andrew, born December 29, 1719.
George Young in Egglesham, a son Andrew, born February 28, 1720.
Jean Kirkland in Eglesham, a son William, born August 16, 1719.
James Train in Evandale, John, born May 8, 1719.
John Morison in Evandale, a son Matthew, born September 12, 1719.
Thomas Hamilton in Evandale, a daughter Margaret, born 27 April 1720.
William Craig in Evandale, a daughter Mary, born March 16, 1720.
James Young in Evandale, a son William, born January 13, 1720.
Alexander Forest in Glasfoord, a son James, born April 16, 1719.
John Muir in Evandale, a daughter Isobel, born October 11, 1719.

At Henselwood, September 18, 1720. Baptized to—
Alexander Martine in Carstares, a son James, born September 2d, 1719.
James Bennet in Carnwath, a daughter Marion, born May 23, 1720.

John Cuthbertson in Dunsyre, a daughter Helene, born June 4, 1720.

James Paton in Carnwath, a daughter Marion, born April 9, 1720.

William Scot in West Calder, a son James, 5 weeks old.

Thomas Weir in Kirknewtown, a daughter Jonet, born December 22, 1719.

Andrew Symington in Carmichal, a son John, born June 22, 1720.

At Caldercrooks, September 25, 1720. Baptized to—

John Walker in Shots, a son William, born November 20, 1719.

John Young in New Monkland, a daughter Marion, born November 1, 1716.

Robert Paterson in Bothwel, a son John, born March 14, 1720.

Archbald Walker in Tarphichen, a daughter Margaret, born June 13, 1720.

James Nilson in Shots, a son Thomas, born the 9 of April 1720.

Jonet Steven in Borrowstounness, a daughter Katharine, born May 13.

John Marshal in Old Monkland, a daughter Margaret, two months old.

John Keddart in Shots, a son John, a month old.

James Stirling in Old Monkland, a daughter Anne, born April 2d, 1720.

William Paterson in Shots, a son William, born December 20, 1719.

John Steil in New Monkland, a daughter Jonet, born January 15, 1719.

John Thomson in Shots, a daughter Jean, born November 17, 1719.

James Gillies in Bothwell, a daughter Margaret, born March 26, 1719.

At Glasgow, September 29, 1720. Baptized to—

William Mitchel in Barony parish, a daughter Jonet, born December 28, 1719.

George Leck in Calder parish, a son Robert, born May 12, 1720.

At Bartonshill, October 1, 1720. Baptized to—

William Scot in Old Monkland, a daughter Jonet, born November 3, 1719.

William Ralton in Calder, a son James, born December 17, 1719.

Alexander Walker in Shots, a son Alexander, born September 29, 1720.

Margaret Cummin, relick to John Stonely in Kilbryde, a son James, 5 quarters of year old.

At Barton'shill, October 4, 1720. Baptized to—
William Stirling in Old Monkland, a daughter Beatrix, born
September 29, 1720.
James Dinning in Barony parish, a daughter Jonet, born
October 18, 1718.
John Selkirk in Old Monkland, a son James, July 3d, 1720.
At Thornhill, October 13th, 1720. Baptized to—
William Cadzin in Kilmadock, a son James, born July 24,
1720.
John Buchanan in Kilmadock, a daughter Margaret, born
July 15, 1720.
William Daunie in Kincarden, a son Thomas, born November 28, 1718.
At . . . ., baptized to James Hastig in Laswade parish a
daughter Elizabeth, born June 9, 1721.
Baptized to James Giffard in Currie parish on July 4, 1722, a
son John, born June 21, 1721 ; October 30, 1726, a
daughter Mary, born January 24, 1726.
At Pentland, August 16, 1725, on Sabbath after sermon, James
Pringle in Dalkieth his son Robert, born . . ., was
baptized by the Rev. Mr. John [M']Millan.
At Crawfurdjohn, May 7, 1721. Baptized to—
Matthew Craig in Evandale, a daughter Jean, one year old.
John M'Clean in Durisdeir, a daughter Margaret, born
March 4, 1721.
At Crawfurdjohn, May 9, 1721. Baptized to—
John Viccars in Lishmahego, a son John, born February 2,
1721.
John Burns in Lishmahego, a son Samuel, born March 16,
1721.
John Paterson in Carnwath, a son James, born March 1,
1721.
Children baptized to Robert Sands in Lieth :—
his daughter Jonet, born February 14, 1705.
his daughter Elizabeth, born September 20, 1708, both
baptized Summer 1709.
his son James, born December 25, 1716, baptized Summer
1718 at Boghall.
his daughter Mary, born October 6, 1714, baptized at Boghall,
Summer 1715.
his son Charles, born January . ., 1718, was baptized at
Thornhill.
his daughter Jean, born March 11, 1720, was baptized
ibidem.
his daughter Margaret, born March 18, 1723, was baptized
at Pentland, September 1, 1723 : all baptized by the
Rev. Mr. John M'Millan.
James Hasty and Shusan Waddel, their children baptized by
the Rev. Mr. John M'Millan :—

baptized December 26, born June 17, 1729, their daughter
Mary.

their son John, born January 9, 1731, baptized Jan. 31, 1731.

their son William and daughter Martha, twins, born August
30, baptized November 28, 1732.

At Crawfoordjohn, March 14, 1722.   Baptized to—

John Reid in Crawfoordmoor, a son Matthew, born August
22, 1721.

John Cockburn in Crawfoordmoor, a daughter Agnes, born
March 9, 1722.

Thomas Reid in Crawfoordmoor, a son William, born January
4, 1722.

John Murdoch in Dowglass, a son John, nine weeks old.

At Crawfoordjohn, July . . . , 1722.   Baptized to—

John Brown in Egglesham, a daughter Marion, born the last
of April 1722.

William Cranston in Crawfoord, a son George, born March
1722.

John Watson in Crawford, a daughter Agnes, February 17,
1722.

David Moffat in Crawfoord, a son Thomas, born March 16,
1722.

John Cuthbertson in Libberton, a daughter Margaret,
March 28, 1722.

Edward Blackstock in Lamington, a son Thomas, born
December 21, 1721.

William Hunter in Crawfoord, a son William, born October
1, 1721.

John Peacock in Colmonell, a daughter Elizabeth, July 30,
1721.

Edward M'Wait in Crawfoord, a daughter Grizel, born April
3, 1722.

At Henselwood, March 18, 1722.   Baptized to—

Robert Dewart in Shots, a son Robert, born June 18, 1721.

Jean Newlands in Shots, Jonet Miller, born February 2,
1721.

Matthew Newlands in Bathgate, a son Robert, born August
25, 1721.

Thomas Watson in Lishmahego, a son Thomas, born September 8, 1721.

James Cuningham in Lanerk, a son William, born March
17, 1722.

John Bryce in Livingston, a son James, born October 1721.

To Bryce Fram in Carluke, a daughter Jonet, born July ult.
1721.

Thomas Telfer in Lishmahego, a son John, born January 28
1721.

John Davie in Carstares, a son John, born March 2d,
1721.

At Henselwood, March 19, 1722.   Baptized to—

Alexander Hamilton in Cambusnethen, a daughter Margaret, [born] February 2, 1721.

Alexander Prentice in Carnwath, a son Alexander, born June ult., 1721.

Alexander Wilson in Carnwath, a son Thomas, born February 16, 1722.

John Gourlay in Biggar, a daughter Martha, [born] August 28, 1721.

Thomas Thomson in Carstares, a son James, born January 4, 1722.

James Dobie in Carluke, a daughter Christian, born January 6, 1722.

John Cunnigham in Carluke, a son Alexander, born January . . ., 1722.

John Dobie in Cambusnethen, a daughter Jonet, born December 28, 1720.

John Morton in Carluke, a son James, born January 7th, 1722.

At Kenmure in Old Monkland, March 25, 1722.   Baptized to—

James Raltoun in Calder, a son William, October 8, 1720; his father William Ralton holding up the child as sponsor.

Andrew Menzies in Barrony parish, a son James, born November . . ., 1719.

Robert Huat in Barony parish, a son William, born February 11, 1721.

William Scot in Old Monkland, a son William, May 23, 1721.

Thomas Duncan in Barony parish, John, March 1721.

James Witherspoon in Old Monkland, a daughter Margaret, born March 1, 1721.

Jane Gardener in Govan, James Freebairn, born February 13, 1721.

James Hay in Easter Linzie, twains, John and Anaple, born February 23, 1721.

William Dobie in Falkirk, William, born February 2, 1721.

James Somervail in Dalzeel, a daughter Sarah, born April 17, 1721.

John Muirhead in Shots, a daughter Margaret [born] August 9, 1720.

At Kenmure, March 25, 1721.   Baptized to—

James Findlay in Barony parish, a daughter Margaret, born October 7, 1720.

John Watson in Newwark, a son James, born September 3, 1719 ; and a daughter Isobel, born July 4, 1721.

William Crawfoord in Newwark, a son James, December ult. 1720.

James Park in Greenock, a daughter Jonet, September 25, 1720.

William Cadzin in Kilmadock, a son William, November 4, 1721.

Robert Thomson in Dalserf, Robert, born October 9, 1720.

John Thomson in Shotts, a son John, born December 25, 1720.

James Rodger in Bothwel, a son William, born May 13, 1721.

James Walker in Shots, a son James, born October 3, 1721.

Thomas Wood in Shots, a son Thomas, born January 12, 1722.

William Masson in Bothwell, a daughter Margaret, December 24, 1720.

John Paterson in Calton of Glasgow, Helene, born January . . ., 1722.

David Selkirk in Barrony, two children, James, born June 7, 1720, and Margaret, born February 25, 1722; William Ralton, his brother-in-law, standing sponsor.

Andrew Young in Nilstoun, a daughter Barbara, born March 17, 1721.

Robert Gardener in Kilmalcom, a daughter Jean, November . . ., 1721.

At Langside Burn, June 19, 1723.—

Robert Scot in Yarrow parish, a son Francis, born February 28, 1723.

William Pot in Cavers parish, a daughter Elizabeth, born March 19, 1723.

James Miller in Hawick, a son John, born April 27, 1723.

George Hyslop in Eskdalemoor, a daughter Elen, May 10, 1723.

John Rae in Eskdalemoor, a daughter Helen, born April 27, 1723; his wife Helen Donaldsone holding up the child.

James Beatie in Westerkirk, a son Francis, age 20 weeks, 1723.

John Grieve in Robertown, a daughter Isobell, born April 26, 1723.

James Hog in Yarrow, a son David, born April 4, 1723.

Walter Black in Yarrow, a daughter Jonet, born April . . ., 1723.

James Bold in Eskdalemoor, a son Thomas, born March 8, 1723.

John Black in Eskdalemoor, a daughter Isobel, born September 29, 1722.

At Crawfoordjohn, August 4th, 1723.—

James Thomson in Crawfoordjohn parish, a son Thomas, born September . . ., 1722.

Thomas Smith in Crawfoordjohn, a daughter Margaret, born
 May . . ., 1723.

John Paul in Kilmarnock, Jonet, born December 16, 1722.

John Moor in Carstairs, Allan, born March 1, 1723.

Robert Prentice in Carluke:—John, born September 16,
 1722.

John Mure in Carluke:—Thomas, born June 22, 1723.

Robert Kennedy in Douglass:—Mary, born November 27
 1722.

James Thomsone in Crawfurdjohn:—Margaret, June 27
 1722.

Thomas Moffat in Crawfoordjohn:—Robert, age 2 years.

John Russel in Old Cumlock:—John, November 1st,
 1722.

John M'Lean in Durisdeer:—Robert, March 24, 1723.

At Crawfoordjohn, August 6th, 1723. Baptized—

John Fallis in Crawfoord:—Margaret, October 13, 1722.

James M'Ewen in Crawfoord:—Jonet, December 1st, 1722.

John Williamson in *Ditto*:—Margaret, December 27, 1722.

James Watson in Crawfoordjohn:—William, January 20,
 1723.

Andrew Symenton in Carmichael:—William, March 10,
 1723.

William Watson in Crawfoordmoor:—Mungo, January 15,
 1723.

Adam Dickson in Glenholm:—Helen, November 10, 1722.

George Porteous in Crawfoordjohn:—Barbara, Agust 6,
 1723.

James Menzies in Crawfordmoor:—Margaret, March 25,
 1723.

Thomas Harknes in Crawfoordmoor:—Agnes, January 1,
 1723.

Adam Blaiklaw in Crawfoordmoor:—William, March 7,
 1723.

Thomas Chamley in Crawfoordmoor:—Ann, April 15, 1723.

Mungo Watson in Crawfoordmoor:—John, January 27,
 1723.

At Drumclog, August 11th, 1723. Baptized to—

John Young in Eaglesham:—Andrew, born May 20, 1721.

Robert Woodbur in Lowdoun:—John, March 1, 1723.

John Smith in Lowdoun:—John, July 29, 1723.

Matthew Craig in Gaalston:—Andrew, September 30, 1722.

Thomas Wilson in Hamiltoun:—John, August 26, 1722.

Robert Young in Eaglesham:—Jonet, October 25, 1721.

John Gilmor in Mearns:—Margaret, January 30, 1722.

James Watson in Eaglesham:—Matthew, March . . ., 1723.

John Armour in Carmunnock:—Agnes, June 1, 1723.

Archbald Lambie in Lowdon:—Jean, July . . ., 1723.

William Young in Carmunnock:—Jonet, June 4th, 1723.

Alexander Moore in Evandale :—Martha, April 13, 1723.

James Davidson in Eaglesham :—Robert, October 8, 1722.

Robert Montgomerie in Eaglesham :—Margaret, March 20, 1723.

John Richmond in Auchinleck :—John, December 4, 1722.

Hugh Smith in Mauchline :—Margaret, April . . ., 1722.

John Lambie in Moorkirk :—Jonet, October 16, 1722.

George Lambie in Dalgeen :—James, August 28, 1722.

Jean Kirkland in Eaglesham :—Robert Wilson, June 9, 1722, the mother holding up the child.

James Young in Evandale : -Isobel, born January 24, 1723.

James Martin in Cambusnethen :—Ann, December 15, 1722.

Robert Thomson in Dalserf :—John, July 5, 1723.

James Tais in Stonehouse :—Alexander, August 18, 1722.

Gawin Rowat in Stonehouse :—Grissel, July 25, 1722.

William Waylie in Moorekirk :—Jean, January 24, 1723.

At Barton'shill, August 18, 1723.   Baptized to—

John Watson in Eaglesham :—Robert, born June 6, 1723.

Robert Howat in Barronie parish :—Margaret, February 13, 1723.

James Ralton in Cather :—Robert, June 2d, 1723, his father, William Ralton, as sponsor, holding up the child.

John Marshal in Old Munklane :—Agnes, July 24, 1722.

Thomas Duncan in Barronie parish :—James, May 9, 1722.

William Ralton in Cather :—Jean, April 15, 1722.

John Scot in Cather :—Jean, September 14, 1722.

James Stirline in Old Monkland :—Mary, December 8, 1722.

James Wotherspoon in Old Monkland :—Jonet, May 23, 1723.

John Selkirk in Old Monkland :—Gavin, February 6, 1723.

James Maxwel in Rutherglen :—Marion, April 8, 1722.

William Greenlaw in Easter Quarter paroch of Glasgow :—Elizabeth, December 29, 1722.

George Young in Nilston :—Jean, November 29, 1722.

John Young in Mearns :—Agnes, May 2d, 1723.

George Russel in Shots :—George, March 9, 1723.

John Muirhead in Shots :—Marion, February 24, 1723.

William Bruce in New Monkland :—Robert, February 1st, 1723.

John Young in New Monkland :—John, October 19, 1722.

Alexander Walker in Shots :—Jean, April 15, 1722.

John Steil in New Monkland :—Jonet, April 26, 1722.

John Gray in Cambusnethen :—Elizabeth, May 8, 1722.

John Dobie in Cambusnethen :—Margaret, February 15, 1723.

Archibald Davidson in Shots :—Mary, October 4, 1722.

William Steven in Glasgow :—Daniel, December 21, 1720 ; and Isobell, June 30, 1723.

James Finlay in Barronie Parish :—William, June 8, 1723.

Robert Paterson in Bothwel :—James, November 25, 1722.

Gavin Moir in Bothwel :—James, May 15, 1722.

James Hay in Easter Linzie :—Jonet, October 17, 1722.

At Devills-Glen, August 21, 1723. Baptized to—

William Aitken in Enderskip :—Margaret, born August 2, 1723.

William Crawfoord in Newport :—William, April 14, 1723.

. Robert Kennedy in Crawfoordsdyke :—Samuel, March 1st, 1720.

At Noristoun, August 25, 1723. Baptized to—

Mr. Alexander Marshal in Kincarden :—George, born June 14, 1723.

James Fleming in Gargunnock :—Jonet, January 14, 1722.

Alexander Wright in Kincarden :—Dorothy, March 26, 1721 ; and James, February 4, 1723.

John Buchanan in Kilmadock :—John, November 3, 1720 ; and Thomas, December 16, 1722.

George Ferrier in Stirline :—Mary, May 8, 1721.

John Faill in St. Ninians :—Ann, August 25, 1722.

William Downie in Kincarden :—Mary, June 20, 1721.

John Galbraith in Balfron :—Robert, November 26, 1722.

William Thomson in Stirline :—Thomas, March 10, 1723.

At Pentland, on a Sabbath day, September 1, 1723, after sermon, a son to Mr. Charles Umpherstoun in Pentland, baptized John, by the Rev. Mr. John M'Millan ; witnesses, James Currie, merchant in Pentland, John Steil there.

At Crafoord John, August 2, 1724, were married by the Rev. Mr. John M'Millan, James Rankin and Martha M'Neil.

At Pentland, their daughter Beatrix, born June 21, 1725 ; *Ibid.*, May 28, 1727, their daughter Mary, born Jan. 24, 1727 ; *Ibid.*, January 31, 1731, their son John, born October 6, 1730 ; were all baptized by the Rev. Mr. John M'Millan.

John Grieve in Eskdale his children baptized by the Rev. Mr. John M'Millan :—

1. His daughter Bethea, born March 31, 1711, was baptized at Killburn after publick sermon next May.

2. His daughter Isobel, born May 1, 1713, baptized *ibidem* after lecture next June.

3. His son Robert, born October 3d, 1716, baptized *ibidem* after sermon, January thereafter.

4. His daughter Jonet, born September 15, 1718, baptized *ibidem* after lecture on November thereafter.

5. His son Walter, born March 2d, 1721, baptized after sermon May next, *ibidem*, viz. at Killburn.

6. His daughter Isobel, born April 26, 1723, baptized next June after sermon at Yeilrigg.

7. His son John, born October 25, 1725, baptized after sermon, April 1726, *ibidem*.

8. His son James, born December 16, 1727, baptized after sermon, June 1728, *ibidem*.

9. His son Thomas, born December 23, 1729, baptized after sermon, April 1730, at Johnston.

10. His son Adam, born May 30, 1731, baptized after lecture May 1732, at Fingland.

11. His daughter Rachel, born September 28, 1733, baptized after sermon, May 1734, at Crurie.

William Grieve and Janet Scot, married by the Rev. Mr. John M'Millan, June 13, 1715; their children baptized by the same Mr. John M'Millan :—

1. James, aged 4 months, baptized after lecture at Craigirigg, January 1717.

2. John, aged 8 months, baptized after sermon at Lanshawburn, August 1718.

3. Margaret, aged 14 weeks, baptized after lecture *ibidem*, July 1719.

4. Elizabeth, aged 8 months, baptized after sermon, *ibid.*, July 1723.

5. Walter, aged 4 months, baptized after lecture, *ibid.*, July 1724.

6. Robert, aged 3 days, baptized after lecture, *ibid.*, October 1725.

7. David, aged 4 months, baptized after lecture at Whitup, June 1727.

8. Hanna, aged 11 months, baptized after sermon at Fingland, July 1729.

9. Barbara, aged one year and 10 months, baptized *ibidem* after sermon, May 1734.

10. Bethea, aged 3 months, baptized after sermon at Crurie, June 1734.

At Sanqhair, June 1, Sabbath, 1724. Baptized to—
Edward Blackstock in Lammington :—James, born January 8, 1724.

Adam French in Crawfoordmoor :—Thomas, October 7, 1723.

Alexander Weir in Crawfoordmoor :—George, March 27, 1724.

At Crawfoordjohn, August 2d, 1724. Baptized to—
William Symentoun in Leshmehago :—William, born January 6, 1724.

James Johnstone in Crawfoordjohn :—Bessie, December 20, 1723.

James Russel in Crawfoordjohn :—Marion, March 10, 1724.

Andrew Blaick in Tweedmoor :—Andrew, April 20, 1724.

John Cuthbertson in Libberton :—Thomas, April 25, 1724.

At Henshilwood in Carnwath, August 9, 1724. Baptized to—
Mrs. Clerk in Kilmadock :—Dorothy, born March 16, 1724.

James Thomson in Shots :—Michael, February 19, 1724.

William Allan, in Old Monkland :—Jame[s], aged 10 weeks, 1724.

James Walker in Shots :—Robert, February 22, 1722.

Thomas Weir in Ratho :—Margaret, October 1st, 1723.

William Symmer in Barronie :—Elizabeth, November 1st, 1723.

William Scot in Calder :—Robert, July 25, 1723.

William Cadzine in Kilmadock :—Alexander, March 20, 1724.

James Currie in Inverlethen :—Walter, October 14, 1723.

James Cairns in Traquair :—John, February 26, 1724.

At Crawfoordjohn, May 29, 1725. Baptized to—

John Williamson in Crawfoordmoor, William, born October 24, 1724.

Crawfoordjohn, May 30, 1725. Baptized to—

Thomas Smith in Crawfoordjohn :—Marion, born May 18, 1725.

Edward M'Watt in Crawfoordmoor :—John, March 16, 1725.

James French in Crawfoordmoor :—Thomas, May 15, 1725.

At Kippoch in Barronie Paroch, June 22, 1725. Baptized to—

Mr. Alexander Marshall in Kincarden :—Hugh, born May 14, 1725.

William Downie in *Ditto* :—Helen, February 1st, 1725.

Alexander Wright in *Ditto* :—Joseph, December 24, 1724.

John Buchanan in Kilmadock :—Joseph, November —, 1724.

James Fleeming in Gargunnock :—John, October —, 1724.

At Moffethills in Shots Paroch, May 21, 1727. Baptized to—

William Robertson in Hamiltone Paroch :—James, 3 quarters age.

Robert Paterson in Bothwel :—Margaret, ½ year old.

John Thomson in Shots :—Jonet, February 2d, 1726.

William Davie in Carnwath :—Bessie, November 17, 1726.

William Thomson in Stirline :—Jean, July 2d, 1725.

John Marshall in Monkland :—John, February 15, 1727.

Thomas Russel in Shots :—Thomas, January 20, 1727.

John Crawfoord in *Ditto* :—Thomas, November 12, 1726.

James Fleming in Gargunnock :—William, March 15, 1727.

John Buchanan in Kilmadock :—Moses, February 15, 1727.

William Adam in *Ditto* :—John, January 21, 1726.

John Fail in St. Ninians :—John, May 17, 1726.

Alexander Wright in Kilmadock :—Margaret, March 7, 1727.

William Smith in Bothwell :—Margaret, quarter old ; Alexander Smith, sponsor.

At Noristoun, March 30, 1728. Baptized to—

William Adam in Kilmadock :—Alexander, born January 15, 1728.

William Cadzine in *Ditto* :—Jonet, December 20, 1728.

At Pentland, on a week day after lecturing for some time, a daughter to Mr. Charles Umpherstoun in Pentland, baptized Elizabeth, by the Reverend Mr. John M'Millan,

3

the 22 of Aprile 1728, before witnesses, James Currie, merchant in Pentland, John Steil there.

Crawfoordjohn, October 27, 1728. Baptized to—

Alexander Weir in Crawfoordmoor :—William, born June 15, 1728.

John M'Aul in Lammingtone :—William, October 14, 1727.

John Martine in Moffet :—Jonet, June . . ., 1728.

At Douglass, February 16, 1729. Baptized to—

Walter Paterson in Crawfoordmoor :—Walter, born January 20, 1729.

James Watson in Crawfoordjohn :—Frances, June 29, 1728.

An Account of Persons married and children baptized by the Reverend Mr. John M'Millan within the Correspondance of Nithsdale from the year 1707 to 1735.

At   , January 12, 1707, were baptized by the Rev. Mr. John M'Millan, minister of the gospel, about 38 persons following :—

1. Margaret Watson, lawfull daughter to the deceast Thomas Watson and Janet M'Kaig, aged 15 years, giving account of her faith and principles herself, and being in fellowship.

2. Jean Ferguson, lawfull daughter to John Ferguson and Margaret Watson in Drumcross, aged 7 years.

Baptized to parents in fellowship.—

To John Mundell in Torthorwald Parish, 4 children, viz., Janet, aged 12 ; Robert, aged 10 ; John, aged 8 ; William, aged 2 years.

To Luke Frizell in Kirkmaho Parish, 5 children, viz., Elspet, aged 10 ; Marion, aged 8 ; John, aged 6 ; Francis, aged 4 ; Katharine, aged 2 years.

To John M'Millan in Kirkmaho Parish, 2 children, viz., Sarah, aged 4 years ; Anna, aged 2 years.

To John Edgar in Tinwald Parish, 3 children, viz., Thomas, aged 16 ; Sarah, aged 14 ; Helen, aged 2 years.

To Herbert Wells in Tinwald Parish, 3 children, viz., James, aged 15, born August 15, 1691 ; Agnes, born April 9, 1700 ; Marion, born November 22, 1703.

To Jean Bell in the same parish, 2 children, viz., Mary, aged 11 ; Sarah, aged 9 years.

To William Edgar in the same parish, 3 children, viz., Mary, aged 14 ; John, aged 8 ; Jean, aged 1 year.

To parents not in fellowship.—

To Adam Cowan in the same parish of Tinwald, 2 children, viz., Agnes, aged 13 ; Marion, aged 10 years.

To John Black in Tinwald parish, 5 children, viz., William, Helen, Robert, Marion, Elspet ; no account of their ages.

To Sarah Bell in the same parish, 3 children, viz., John Ranning, aged 15; Mary, aged 12; William, aged 6 years.

To William Mathison in Gretnay Parish, 3 children, viz., Grizel, born March 24, 1701; John, born February 8, 1703; and Janet, born April 14, 1705.

John Miller in Dryfe, aged 16 years, who answered for himself, his father not being permitted.

At the Burn of Tinwald, January 19, 1707, were married by the said Mr. John M'Millan :—

Thomas Henderson and Janet Mathison; Adam Glessell and Jean Wright; William Black and Janet Bell; William Beck and Mary Halliday; John Edgar and Rosina Corrie.

At   , January 13th, 1707, were married *ab eodem*:—Samuel Clark and Mary Wilson; James Scot and Janet Black.

April 25, 1707, were married :—
John Watson and Helen M'Kaig.

At Burn of Tinwald, May 5, 1707, were married by the said Mr. M'Millan :—

William Duthie and Elspet Maxwell; Andrew Corbet and Barbara Cowan; John Bell and Janet Dempster; John Frizel and Janet Porter; Archibald Grieve and Janet Henderson.

At Pollet Hill, October 6, 1707, were married by the foresaid minister :— George Henderson and Mary Glover; Christopher Calvert and Janet Bell; James Carsell and Agnes Graham.

October 13, 1707, at Balmagie, were married *ab eodem* :—
James Clerk and Agnes Mundel.

At Heazelberrie, October 12, 1707, was baptized *ab eodem* :—
John Knox, son to James Knox in Cummertrees parish.

February 3, 1708, was baptized by the said Mr. M'Millan :—
Mary Mundell, daughter to the deceast Robert Mundel in Runnerhead.

February 5, 1708, were baptized *ab eodem* :—
Robert Douglas in Birkhill, his eldest son James; Archbald Grieve, smith at   , his eldest son John; John Edgar, younger, his eldest son John; William Beck in Hartbush, his daughter Janet. No account of their age.

Eodem die, were married by the said Mr. John M'Millan :—
James Paton and Jean Coupland; Robert Mundel and Mary Ranning; Mathew Short and Isobel Brown; Thomas Frizel and Janet Wilson.

At Crafoordjohn, February 9, 1708, were married *ab eodem*, William Crosby and Janet Craik.

May 5, 1708, were baptized by the Rev. Mr. John M'Millan :—
Andrew Wells in Kilpatrick Juxta, his daughter Rebecka;

and on the next day, John Stinston, rather Stevenson, in the parish of Hoddam, his daughter Mary.

At Glenmade, January 2, 1709, were baptized *ab eodem* :—
Robert Mundell in Dalrusken, his eldest daughter Janet.
John Frizel in Fullton, his eldest daughter Margaret.
John M'Millan in Dincow, his son John.

January 12, 1710, was baptized *ab eodem ministro Evangelii* :—
James Knox in Cummertrees, his daughter Mary.

December *ult.*, 1708, was baptised by the Rev. Mr. John M'Millan * :—
William Black, his son John, in the first year of his age.

January 3, 1709, were married, David Jardon of Goosgreen and Marion Laidlay ; John Kenaday and Grizel Tait.

At Birkhill, January 4, 1709, were married, Samuel Cowan and Isobel Brand ; Edward Beck and Margaret Halliday ; James Wilkin and Rebecka Paterson ; Thomas Brown and Jean Gillespie.

On the same day, was baptized, Luke Frizel, in Glenmade his son Luke, aged 1 year.

· At Park, April 25, 1709, were married, Thomas Atchison and Janet Linton ; James Mundell and Agnes Gass.

At Burn of Tinwald, April 26, 1709, were married, James Cowan and Mary Watson ; William Duff and Janet Parton.

At Marjorie Muirside, April 28, 1708, were married, James Paterson in Tinron and Isobel Mathison in Closeburn.

At Runnerhead of Tinwald, September 28, 1708, were baptized, William Beck in Hartbush his son John ; John Frizel his eldest son John ; Alexander Wilson his son John.

At Tinwald, January 8, 1710, were baptized, James Wilkin in Kirkmaho parish, his eldest daughter Margaret ; Edward Beck in Tinwald parish, his eldest daughter Jean.

At Burn of Tinwald, January 9, 1710, was baptized, Thomas Gillespie in Closeburn parish, his son George.

At Kilburn, January 16, 1710, was baptized David Jarden in the parish of Aplegirth, his eldest son John.

At the same place and on the same day, were married, Thomas M'Vittie and Jean Lawson, both in parish of Kirkmichaell ; John Carsell in Wamphrey parish and Janet Bettie in Kilpatrick Juxta.

At Windshields, January· 17, 1710, were married, John Henry in Wamphrey parish and Jean Graham in Hutton parish.

At Balmagie, January 24, 1710, were married, John Newlands and Helen Lowrie, both in Kirkmaho parish.

At   , January 12, 1709, was baptized, George Henderson in parish of Hoddam his eldest son James, born October 1708.

* His name occurs before almost every entry after this time, and is herefore hereafter omitted to avoid needless repetition.

January 12, 1710, was baptized, Christopher Colvert in
Hoddam parish, his eldest daughter Jean.

The Obligation of Robert Goldie in Closeburn parish for and
anent his scandall of leaving the Testimony of Christ Jesus
and complying with the defections of the present times, and
this he did before he could have the benefite of baptism for
his child, which is as follows :—I, undersubscriber, out of
the sight and sense of my wayes since I left the Meeting,
cause and way of God, do hereby testifie against the same
and myself for going on therein, and that with reference
both to Church and State as now circumstantiated, hereby
giving it under my hand to be answerable (if alive) to the
first faithfull judicatorie of Church or State capable to judge
or determine anent the censure to be inflicted according to
the degree of the offence ; and both as to hearing such as
in duty I was not oblidged to hear or joyn with, and some
years ago owning and acknowledging the present corrupt
magistrates by paying of publick impositions to them, &c.
All which I promise to do, or quhatever else can be laid
to my charge as censurable or punishable, as witness my
hand before these witnesses, John Mathison and James
Paterson. *Sic Subscribitur*, ROBERT GOLDIE; John
Mathison, witness ; James Paterson, witness. At Kirkland-
head of Dalgairnoch, April 30, 1709.

At   , January 29, 1711, were baptized, John
Crechton in Glencairn parish, his daughter Katharine ;
Archibald Glencross in the parish of Closeburn, his eldest
daughter Mary ; John Watson in Closeburn parish, his
eldest daughter Janet ; James Mathison there, his son
Robert : all within the first year of their age.

At Birkhill, January 30, 1711, were baptized, Robert Douglas
in the parish of Closeburn, her daughter Agnes, born
January 15, 1711.

John Edgar in Tinwald parish, his daughter Jean, born
October 28, 1709.

William Black in Tinwald parish, his son John, aged 1
year.

James Cowan in Kirkmaho, his daughter Jean, born
September 25, 1710.

Luke Frizel there, his daughter Mary, born May 10, 1710;
also James Caruthers, son to Katharine Mundell,
Herbert Wells sponsor.

At   , February 5, 1711, was baptized, Robert
Mundell, his daughter Rebecka, aged 7 months.

At Burn of Tinwald, February 5, 1711, were married, Luke
Frizel and Mary Cowan ; John Barton and Margaret Wells ;
Andrew Glover and Isobel Barton : having all cautioners
for their pawns.

At Eglefechan, February 1, 1711, were baptized, William

Mathison in Lochmeban, his child; Archibald Grieve there, his son Robert, born February 20, 1710.

At   , February 1, 1712, was baptized, George Henderson his daughter Janet, born December 1711.

At Coldens, August 12, 1711, was baptized, John Stinson, weaver, his son John.

At Tinwald, April 27, was baptized, James M'Coons in the parish of Keir, his son Alexander and daughter Sarah; James Paterson and Isobel Mathison, their son Mark, aged   ; William M'Vitie in Kirkmichaell, his son James; Jo: Frizel and Janet Potter; their daughter Rebecka, aged one year; Edward Beck and Margaret Halliday in Tinwald, their daughter Janet, age 1 year; William Beck and Mary Halliday in Tinwald, their son William, of the same age.

At   , April 28, 1712, were baptized, Luke Frizel and Mary Cowan their daughter Janet, born April 17, 1712; Alexander Dove and Janet Edgar in Kirkmaho their son John, born October 15, 1712 (*sic*); and Thomas Edgar, aged the 2d year, but whose son he is I do not find.

At Pellethill, in Hoddam parish, May 5, 1712, were married, James Harkness and Agnes Stoddart; Robert Walker and Margaret Frizell; Alexander Henrie and Margaret Thomson; William Black and Janet Bell;—John Bell caution for all.

May 4, 1712, were baptized, Andrew Wells in Kilpatrick Juxta, his son Joseph, aged 3 months; David Jarden and Marion Laidly in Hutton parish, their son David, aged 18 weeks; James Knox and Marion Rodick their son David aged 6 months; John Rodick and Jean Bell their daughter Helen, aged one month.

At Tinwald, August, 10, 1712, were baptized, Archibald Grieve and Janet Henderson their son Thomas, aged 11 weeks; William M'Vitie his daughter Janet, aged 3 weeks; James Wilkin and Rebecka Paterson in Closeburn their son John, aged 6 months.

At Burnmuir in Closeburn, August 11, 1712, were baptized, John Watson and Helen M'Caig in Closeburn their daughter Helen, aged 7 weeks; James Mathison and Margaret Novison there, their daughter Grizell, aged 5 months.

At Coldens, August 17, 1712, on the Lord's Day were baptized, John Forsyth and Bessie Smellie in Hoddam their son, Jacob, aged 1 month; James M'Vitie and Margaret Aitken in Garrell parish their son James, 6 months; John Mundell and Jean R——— in Torthorwald parish their daughter Mary, aged   .

At Glencross, April 19, 1713, were baptized, Thomas Grierson and Sarah Smith in Kells parish their daughter Margaret, aged 1 year 3 quarters; Samuel Clark and Marion

M'Millan in Dumellington their son James, aged 1½ year; Thomas M'Adam and Margaret M'Giltragh in Glencairn their son James, born August 17, 1712.

At Naughlie Shang, April 23, 1713, were baptized, Robert Douglas and Jean Paton in Closeburn, their son Samuel, born December 11, 1713 (*sic*); Thomas Gillespie and Elspet Thomson there their daughter Isobel, aged 1 year 3 quarters.

Same day and place, were married, James Summer and Jean M'Chine both in the parish of Tinwald.

At Naughle-Shang, April 26, 1713, being the Lord's Day, were baptized, David Moffat in Crawfoord parish his daughter Margaret, aged 6 weeks; James Harkness in Kilpatrick Juxta his son James, aged 9 weeks; Samuel Stewart and Mary Cowan in Tarregls parish their daughter Elizabeth, born November 30, 1712; Mathew Short and Isobel Brown in Moffat their daughter Agnes, aged 4 months; William Spence and Agnes Maxwell in Tinwald parish their daughter Jean, aged 14 years; John Hope in parish of Kilpatrick Juxta his daughter Margaret, aged 3 months; Alexander Wilson and Margaret Mitchel in Johnston parish, their son Mathew, born February 17, 1713; Jo: Frizel and Janet Porter in Kirkmichall parish their daughter Jean, aged 1 month.

At Hartbush, April 28, 1713, were married, William Wells and Margaret Wells; Thomas Edgar and Jean Wilson; Robert Barton and Mary Glover.

On the same day, were baptized, William Duthie and Janet Barton in Torthorwald parish their daughter Mary, born March 8, 1711; Jo: Robson and Janet Maxwell in Tinwald parish, their daughter Janet, born August 27, 1712.

At Coldens, May 3, 1713, were baptized, George Henderson and Mary Glover in Hoddam parish their daughter Gills, born April 11, 1713; William Black and Barbara Henderson in Midleby parish, their daughter Anna, aged 3 months; William Mathison and Jean Hislop there their daughter Bethea, born January 7, 1713.

At   , May 4, 1713, were married, James Proudfoot and Janet Short in parish of Garrell *alias* Kirkmichaell; James Donaldson and Jean Henderson. Next day, married, Robert Grieve and Margaret Donaldson; James Brown and Mary Brown.

At Tinwald, May 6, 1713, were married, William Swan and Helen Frizell.

At Balmagee, August 3, 1713, were married, John Donaldson in Tinwald and Ediz Murray in Dumfriess.

At Hartbush, February 24, 1714, were baptized, John Newlands and Helen Lowrie their daughter Mary, aged one month; Thomas Edgar and Jean Wilson their son David, aged 15 days; William Black and Janet Bell in Tinwald their son

David, aged 13 days; Thomas Brown and Jean Gillespie in Closeburn their son John, aged 18 weeks; Jo: Mundell and Jean Rae in Torthorwald their son Joseph, born July 28, 1713; William Duthie and Janet Parton there their son James, born December 18, 1713; Isobel Frizel, aged 27 days.

At Burn of Tinwald, April 13, 1714, was baptized, William Paterson and Isobel Grierson their daughter Mary, born October 5, 1713.

Ibid., April 12, 1713 (*sic*), James Summer and Jean M'Chine their daughter Jean, born April 2, 1714 (*sic*).

At Coldens, April 18, 1714, were baptized, Cristopher Colvert and Janet Bell in Hoddam parish their son James, born June 3, 1713; Robert Johnston and Margaret Wilson their daughter Jean, born May 31, 1713; David Jarden, Marion Ladlay, their son William, aged 13 weeks 5 days; James Knox and Mary Rodick in Cumbertrees parish, their daughter Agnes, aged 7 or 8 weeks.

At Pellethill, April 19, 1714, were married, Robert Grieve and in the parish of Moffat; Adam Johnston in the same parish and Jean Paterson in Kirkpatrick Juxta; Stephen Boys and Janet Martin in St. Mungo parish.

At Birkhill, March 13, 1715, were baptized, Adam Johnston and Jean Paterson in Moffat their daughter Agnes, aged 7 weeks.

Ibid., on the morrow, William Wells and Margaret Wells their son John, born May 21, 1714; John Frizel and Janet Porter, their son Michael, born March 12, 1714; Robert Barton and Mary Glover their son James, born June 17, 1714; Edward Beck and Margaret Haliday their daughter Jean, born July 31, 1714; Andrew Glover and Isobel Barton their daughter Janet, aged 7 weeks; all in the parish of Tinwald. Luke Frizel and Katherine Gillespie, their son William, born April 27, 1714; Thomas Wightman their (*sic*) daughter Grizel (*sic*); in parish of Kirkmaho.

At Hartbush, March 21, 1715, was baptized, Jo: Edgar, younger, and Rosina Corrie in parish of Tinwald, their daughter Janet.

At Birkhill, March 13, 1715, were baptised, Robert Douglas and Jean Paton in Closeburn their son William, aged 1 month; John Watson and Helen M'Kaig their son John, born February . . ., 1714; Archibald Glencross in Closburn his daughter Janet, aged 3 month.

At Birkhill, March 15, 1715, were married, Alexander Dove and Elspet Wells in Tinwald; William Johnson and Margaret Caruthers in Lochmaban; Jo: Beck and Janet in Closeburn.

At Hartbush, March 22, 1715, were baptised, John Edgar and Rosina Corrie their daughter Janet, in Kirkmaho.

March 27, 1716, *Ibidem*, were baptised, William Swan and Helen Frizel in Kirkmaho their daughter Janet, aged 8 months; William Wells and Margaret Wells in Tinwald their daughter Janet, born November 25, 1715; Thomas Edgar and Jean Wilson their daughter Sarah, born July 5, 1715; William M'Vittie and Jean Brown in Jonston their son William, aged 3 months.

Ibid., April 16, 1716, were baptised, Edward Hastie and Janet Thorburn in Johnston parish their daughter Janet, November 1715.

At the said place, April 2, 1716, were married, Robert Black, elder, and Jean Wells.

At Barnmoor in Closeburn, February 17, 1717, was baptised, James Summer and Jean M'Chine in Closeburn their son James, aged . . . ; Robert Brown in Keir his son Peter, born September 21, 1716; Alexander Niveson and Agnes Milligen in Closeburn their son John, September 19, 1716; James Cowan and Mary Watson in Kirkmaho, their daughter Grizel, born June 11, 1716.

The names of several children baptized about this time at Hartbush and Wolistone are insert already by Mr. Hugh Clark, so it is superfluous to set them down again.

At Walistone, March 17, 1718 (Munday), were married, William Wells and Grizel Robison in Eglefechan.

Ibid., next day, Jo: Hope and Janet Armstrong in parish of Middleby; Reinald Gibson and Margaret Rodick; the last pair married on Wednesday after.

At Hartbush, March 24, 1718, were married, Andrew Caruthers in parish of Drysdale and Nicolas Maxwell in St. Mungo parish.

March 26, William Spence and Margaret Edgar, both in Tinwald.

At Hartbush, June 5, 1720, were baptized, Robert Walker and Agnes Atchison in parish of Hoddam their daughter Margaret, born August 7, 1719; James Knox and Jean Byers in parish of Cummertrees their daughter Jean, born November 30, 1719; Jo: Hope and Janet Armstrong in parish of Middleby their daughter Margaret, born May 20, 1720; Jo: Bell and Rachel Johnston in St. Mungo parish their son Andrew, born November 1719; William Richardson in parish of Lyne his daughter Christian, born January 12, 1720; Adam Johnston and Jean Paterson in Kirkpatrick Juxta their daughter Jean, aged 5 weeks; Adam Dixon, and Jean Hill in parish of Tweedsmoor their son James, aged 5 months; Robert M'Vittie and Janet Eskdale in Garrel parish their son James, aged 7 months; Andrew Wells and Isobel Tod in Kilpatrick Juxta their son Josias, 3 quarters.

At Hartbush, June 6, 1720, were married, William Rodick and Katherine Bell both in parish of Cummertrees;

Christopher Paty and Janet Gillespie in parish of Closeburn; William Laidlay and Janet Hartbush in parish of Moffat; John Jarden and Janet Grhame in parish of Aplegirth.

Ibidem, next day, married, Jo: Kilpatrick and Mary Watson.

On the same day was baptised at Netherhouses of Auchencairn, William Swan and Helen Frizel in parish of Kirkmaho, born May 29, 1720.

At Hartbush, July 23, 1721, were baptised, James Cowan and Mary Watson in Kirkmaho their son James, born March 10, 1721; Robert M'Vittie and Janet Eskdale in the same parish their son Thomas, born April 19, 1721; Thomas Edgar and Jean Burges in Tinwald, their daughter Jean, born May 28, 1721; Agnes Barton in Tinwald, born April 13, 1721.

At Hartbush, November 7, 1721, were baptised, Christopher Paty and Janet Gilespie in Closeburn their son John, born August 24, 1721; Luke Frizel and Mary Cowan in Kirkmaho their daughter Elspet, aged 9 months.

At Hartbush, May 31, 1722, were baptized, Andrew Wells and Isobel Tod in Johnston parish their son Josias, aged 6 weeks; Mathew Short and Isobel Broun in Moffat their daughter Margaret, born April 6, 1722; James Graham and Mary Wilson in Garrel parish their son Joseph, born February 6, 1722; Archibald Glencross in Kilpatrick his daughter Jean, born May 16, 1722; Thomas Kilpatrick and Jean Thomsone in Kirkmaho, their son Archibald, aged 6 months; Jo: Edgar, elder, and Jean Corrie in Kirkmaho, their son Joseph, born February 3, 1722; Edward Beck and Margaret Halliday in Tinwald, their son William, aged six months.

At Dalveen in Durisdeer parish, June 5, 1722, were baptised, James Hislop his son Joseph; William Thomson his daughter Agnes; William Dickson his daughter Jean; James Williamson his daughter Mary; John Harknes his son James; all in the parish of Crafoord. James Muncie his son John, in Durisdeer parish; all born in year 1722.

At Hartbush, June 30, 1723, were baptised, Joseph Craig and Janet M'Vittie in Kirkmichael parish their daughter Jean, born August 1722; Jo: Kirkpatrick and Anna Clark in Kirkmichael their son Robert born July 9, 1722; William Black and Janet Bell in Kirkmaho their son James, aged 3 years; Jo: Brown and Jean Broun in Kirkmichael their daughter Isobel, aged 1 year; John Hope and Agnes Johnston in Moffat parish their son John; Thomas Edgar and Jean Burges in Tinwald their daughter Agnes, born April 6, 1723; William Spence and Margaret Edgar their daughter Jannet; James Stiel and Agnes Fade their daughter Agnes, born April 15, 1723; Robert Lourie and

Janet Corrie their daughter Isobel, born October 20, 1723; John M'Millan and Marion Glendoning in Sanqhair their daughter Elspet, aged 8 weeks; John Paterson and Jean Ker in Kilbride parish their son Walter, aged 6 months; William Aitken and Janet Howetson in Kilbride their son William, aged 6 months; John Howetson and Agnes Kerr in Kilbride their daughter Agnes, aged 4 months; David Watson and Elspet Jackson in their son John, aged 5 weeks; Richard Irving and Mary Forrester in their son . . ., aged 5 weeks; Alexander Halliday and Jean Fleeming in Kirkmaho parish their daughter Jean, aged 6 months.

At Hartbush, July 1, 1723, were baptised, John Watson and Helen M'Kaig in parish of Closeburn their daughters Agnes, born January 1, 1720, Margaret, born May 31, 1722; Joseph Mundel in Tinwald his son James, born June 30, 1723; David Corrie and Janet Corrie in Tinwald their daughter Bessie, June 30, 1723; Samuel Cowan and Mary Bell in Tinwald their daughter Janet, aged 3 years; James Cowan and Mary Watson in Kirkmaho their daughter Janet, born June 30, 1723.

Ibidem, July 12,—Matthew Short his son Mathew, aged 4 months.

At Hartbush, July 14, 1724, were baptized, John Bratten in Tinwald his two children, John and Janet, aged 9 months; Robert Mundel his son Robert, aged 11 months; William Spence and Margaret Edgar in Tinwald their son John, aged 6 months; James Charters his son John, aged 6 months; James M'Gown his son John, aged 4 months; John Nicolson his son Benjamin, aged one year; John Brand in Tinwald his daughter Agnes, born November 4, 1723; James Brand there his daughter Janet, aged 9 months; Christopher Patie and Janet Gillespie their daughter Agnes, born May 17, 1724; John Forsyth in his daughter Elizabeth, aged one year 11 months; Luke Frizel in Kirkmaho his son Thomas, aged 9 months; John Wells and Janet Halliday in Tinwald their daughter Jean, born July 4, 1724.

At Crafoord John, August 3, 1724, were married, Alexander Halliday and Elspet Frazer in Tinwald. [*Ni fallor*]

At Hartbush, May 3, 1725, were baptised, John Nicolson in . . . his son Jonah, born December 25, 1724; John Forsyth in . . . his son James, born July 17, 1724; Thomas Kilpatrick in his daughter Jean, born April 10, 1725; Alexander Smith in his son David, born March 6, 1725; Robert Lourie in his son James, born March 26, 1725; John Muncy of Garrick his daughter Helen, born April 25, 1724; John Kilpatrick in Kirkmichael his daughter Margaret, December 29, 1724; Robert M'Vittie in his daughter Jannet, born January 15, 1724; James Grahame in his son James, born December 11, 1724; John Brown in his daughter Jannet, born March 3, 1725; William Bran in his son Robert, born March 22, 1724.

At , October 10, 1725, was baptized, Alexander Halliday and Elspet Fraizer their daughter Katharine, May 24, 1725.

At Hartbush, April 13, 1726, were baptized, Thomas Edgar in . . . his daughter Janet, aged 16 days; John Watson in Barns Moor his daughter Honorat (? Henorat), born July 31, 1725; Thomas Harkness in his son Thomas, born February 14, 1726; John Craig in his son Thomas, born November 22, 1725; James Patterson in his daughter Helen, born November 20, 1725; David Watson in his son David, aged 3 months; John Cavort in his daughter Janet, aged 3 months; William Charters in his son James, born June 1, 1725; William Young in his son William, aged 3 years, and daughter Jean, born November 1725; James Harkness in his daughter Isobel, born December 15, 1725; Christopher Pattie (in) his daughter Janet, born February 25, 1726; James Muncy his son Robert, aged 6 weeks; James Minize his daughter Janet, aged 2 months; William Atken his daughter Margaret, born December 31, 1725; William Brand his daughter Jean, aged 8 weeks 4 days; John Kilpatrick his son George, aged 6 months.

At Hartbush, July 9, 1727, were baptised, John Mitchell in Johnston parish his son James, aged 9 months; Adam Johnston *ibidem* his son James, aged 8 weeks; Luke Frazer in Kirkmaho parish his daughter Sarah, aged one year; Robert Fisher in Tinwald parish his son James, aged 2 years; Robert Bratton in his daughter Marion, born November 30, 1726; Andrew Wells and Isobel Tod their daughter Elizabeth, aged 9 months; John Muncy in Garick his son Robert, aged 11 months; William Russel in Garrel parish, his daughter Sarah, born March 7, 1725; Thomas Kilpatrick in Kirkmaho his son John, born June 6, 1727; Robert Laurie *ibidem*, his son Robert, born December 24, 172 . . ; David Glendoning in Kirkmaho parish his son John, aged 6 months; James Cowan in Kirkmaho parish his daughter Jean, born June 30, 1727; Joseph Mundel in Tinwald his daughter Jannet, born April 23, 1727; Francis Johnston in Closeburn his daughter Helen, born January 30, 1726; James Graham in Kirkmichal his daughter Margaret, born June 30, 1727; Robert M'Vittie *ibid.*, his son John, born December 20,

1726; Robert Short in Kirkmichael, his son John, born March 29, 1727; David Corrie in Tinwald his son John, aged 11 months.

At Hartbush, July 11, 1727, were baptized:—James Brand in Tinwald his son William, aged 9 months; John Mundel in Torthorwald his daughter Margaret, aged 11 years; his son Benjamin, aged one year 6 months; William Spence in Tinwald his daughter Jean, born October 28, 1726.

At Naughtieshang, July 13, 1727, were baptized:—John Brown in his daughter Jean, aged 3 years; James Johnston in Garrel parish his daughter Anna, aged 10 days; Alexander Halliday in Kirkmaho his daughter Janet, born December 29, 1726; James Patie in Closburn his five children, Elizabeth, aged 10 years; Anna, aged 8 years; Jean, aged 5 years; John, aged 2 years; Agnes, aged 4 days.

At Hartbush, July 10, 1727, were married, Edward Sittelinton and Mary M'Fegan in Dunscore; soon after at the Manse of Balmagie, John Crosbie and Jean M'Vittie.

At Amesfield, June 29, 1729, was baptized, James Brand in . . . his daughter Mary.

At Hartbush, June 30, 1729, were baptized, James Mundel and Agnes Gass in Tinwald their son John, giving an account of his faith took on the engagements himself, aged 18 years; John M'Millan in Sanquair parish his son Alexander, aged 4 weeks; Alexander Smith, *ibid.*, his son William, born December 29, 1728; John Grierson in Glencairn his daughter Janet, born March 10, 1729; John Hair in Holywood parish his daughter Elizabeth, born October 20, 1728; Edward Sittelinton in Dunscore his son John, born July 20, 1728; John Cavour in Annandale his daughter Jean, born March 12, 1729; James Gass at Dutton his daughter Agnes, born April 18, 1729; Robert Brand in Tinwald his son William, born February 17, 1729; Robert Mundel in Kirkmichael his son Alexander, January 12, 1729; John Forsyth in his daughter Jean, aged 3 months; James Adamson in Kirkmichael his son James, born January 8, 1729; William Brand in Kirkmaho his son James, born 7 of April, 1729; William Charters *ibid.*, his daughter Mary, born November 18, 1727; Robert Lourie in Tinwald his son John, February 27, 1729; Alexander Halliday in Kirkmaho his son John, March 27, 1729; "other three children are mentioned, but their names are not insert."

At Hartbush, May 29, 1729, were baptized, Thomas Henderson in Dunscore his son John, born April 14, 1729; William Muirhead in Glencairn his son Robert, born May 23, 1729; Thomas Henderson in Midlbie his son William, born December 28, 1728; Robert Walker in Hoddam his son Nathaniel, born January 27, 1729; William Kirkpatrick in

Kirkmaho, his son James, July 23, 1728; Robert Fisher in Tinwald. his son John, aged 4 months; Robert M'Vittie in Garrel his daughter Jean, born January 9, 1729; William Ruddock in Cummertrees parish his daughter Janet, aged 8 weeks; James Johnston in Garrel parish his daughter Mary, born May 3, 1729.

At Dalveen, May 30, 1729, were baptized, John Muncie in Closeburn his son William, aged 8 weeks; James Gibson in parish of Durisdeer, his son Robert, aged 2 months.

At Hartbush, May 21, 1732, were baptized, Alexander Halliday in Kirkmaho, his sons Thomas, born February 18, 1730, and William, born October 8, 1731; Luke Frazer, *ibid.*, his daughter Elizabeth, aged one year; David Glendoning in Kirkmaho his daughter Marion, July 3, 1731; Robert Lourie *ibid.*, his daughter Agness, born August 2, 1730; Joseph Mundel in Tinwald his daughter Rebecca, born June 25, 1731; James Johnston in Garrel parish his daughter Mary, born November 17, 1731; John Brown in Kirkmichael his daughter Mary, born December 11, 1730; David Watson in Johnston parish his daughter Jean, born September 14, 1731; Thomas Edgar in Tinwald his son Thomas, born October 14, 1729; James Kinneel in Tongland parish his son William, aged one year; James Tait in   his daughter Jean, born April 28, 1730; James Brand minor, in Tinwald, his son Robert, born November 20, 1729; James Adamson in Kirkmichal his son Robert, September 1, 1730; William Muirhead in Glencairn his daughter Agness, December 31, 1731; John M'Clymount in Colmonel parish his daughter Agness, aged 2 years; Hugh M'Geore in parish of Orr his son William, aged one year 6 months; Edward Crocket in Lochruton parish his daughter Mary, aged one year 9 months; Edward M'Olnea in Parton parish his daughter Janet, born October 7, 1731; James Brand in Tinwald his daughter Janet, March 17, 1729; Alexander Gordon in   his daughter Marion, aged one year 9 months; Robert M'Vittie in Garrel his daughter Margaret, born August 8, 1731; William Spence in Tinwald his son William, born August 1, 1729; John Edgar in Tinwald his son John, aged 5 months; William Watson his daughters Jean, aged   ; Mary, born April 17, 1731; William Brand in Kirkmaho his daughter Katharine, March 11, 1730; William Brand (*an alius an idem nescio*) in   his son John, aged 4 months; Mary Mundel, daughter to the deceast James Mundel in Tinwald, gave an account of her faith herself, as also did William Duffie in Torthorald his daughter Isobel aged   ; Christopher Patie in Closeburn his son George,

aged 8 weeks ; James Patie in   his son James,
born April 4, 1731.

"The children's names baptized summer 1733 by Mr.
M'Millan are not here insert, Mr. Marshal being with him got the
account."

At Hartbush, June 15, 1735, were baptized :—James Hair-
stons in Glencairn, John, 16 weeks; Jo: Grier his
daughter Nicolas, aged 5 months; Andrew Frazer in
Clos[?burn], Andrew, aged 8 weeks; Jo: Forsyth in
Mousel, Joseph, 6 months ; Alexander Holliday, Kirkmaho,
Francis, February 17, 1735 ; Adam Minize in Kirkmichael,
Catharine, May 1, 1734.

At Knock, June 18, 1735, after lecture, week day, were
baptised, William Thoreburn his child ; David Watson his
child; both in Johnston.

At Hartbush, June 12, 1735, were married, Thomas Edgar and
Jean Johnston ; and on the 17 day, John Bell and
Margaret Wells ; William Ranning and Agnes Johnston.

At Shank, about 8 days after, were married, Christopher Armstrang and Mary Litster.

At Crurie in Eskdale, July 1733, were baptized by the Rev.
Mr. John M'Millan, minister of the Gospel, James Hog in
Yara parish, his daughter Janet, born December 25, 1732;
Adam Linton in   his daughter Janet, born March
13, 1734; Ja: Henry in Eskdalemuir his son John, born
February 20, 1734.

At Fingland, July 1736, were baptized by the Rev. Mr.
M'Millan, William Hislop his son William, born November
16, 1734; James Miller in   his daughter Helen,
born March 8, 1734; Jo: Little in   his daughter
Bessy, born April 4, 1734; Jo: Harkness in   his
daughter Bessy, born October 5, 1734; Robert Anderson
in   his son James, born January 4, 1735; Robert
Armstrang in   his daughter Helen, born   ;
Andrew Black in   his son James, born
1733; James Halliday in Eskdalemuir his son William ;
Adam Linton in the same parish his [son] Thomas; Jo:
Robertson in the parish of Etreck his daughter Janet.

At Eldinhope, July 1736, on Sabbath after sermon, were
baptized, William Laidlaw in Etreck parish his son
William, born December 1735; Alexander Hislop in
Yara parish his daughter Bessy, born January 1736; James
Hog in Yara parish his son James, born March 1736;
Thomas Telfer in the parish of Eskdalemuir his son Jo:,
born March 1736.

At Crurie, June 8, 1738, were baptized, John Grieve in Eskdalemoor parish his son William, born May 1738; James
Henry in the said parish his daughter Helen, born April
1738; Adam Linton in   his daughter Isobel, born

May 1738 ; George Knox in   his daughter Sara, born
July 7, 1737 ; Thomas Armstrong in   his daughter
Mary, aged one year 6 months ; James Halliday in Eskdalemuir his son Samuel, born April 1, 1738 ; Peter Grahame
in Hutton parish his son John, born July 7, 1737.

At Monherick near Crafoordjohn, on the 9th of November
1735, before sermon in the afternoon were baptized by the
Rev. Mr. John M'Millan :—

James Witherton, his son James, born May 26, 1735 ;
Alexander Williamson his son Robert, born
September 1st, 1735 ; John M'Millan his
daughter Margaret, aged 9 weeks ; all living in
the parish of Sanquar. Thomas Reid his son
Thomas, born September 7, 1735 ; Archbald
Edgar, his daughter Jean, born August 16, 1735 ;
in parish of Crafoord.

At Crafordjohn, on the 10th of November 1735, after lecture,
was baptized by the Rev. Mr. John M'Millan :—John Blaik
his son Peter, born October 29, 1735 ; in Parish of Crafoord.

At Braehead, November 30, 1735, after sermon on Sabbath,
was baptized, Robert Turnbul his son Mathew, born
October 27, 1735, living in the parish of New Monkland.

At Breahead, January 11, 1736, after sermon, was baptized, by
the Rev. Mr. John M'Millan :—Robert Ingles his daughter
Janet, born November 7, 1735, living in Glasgow.

At Braehead, March 14, 1736, after sermon, was baptized,
John Scot and Margaret Langmure their daughter Mary,
born November 25, 1735, living in the parish of Calder
near Glasgow.

At Braehead, March 21, 1736, after sermon on the Sabbath,
was baptized, Charles Brown and Margaret Clarkson, their
daughter Helen, born November 6, 1735, living in the
parish of Carnwath.

At Braehead, April 18, 1736, on Sabbath, after sermon, was
baptized, Jean Hamilton, born March 25, 1736, daughter
to Gavin Hamilton and Jean Allan in Hamilton parish.

At Braehead, May 2ᵈ, 1736, on the Sabbath after sermon,
were baptized, Robert Ingles in Douglas, his daughter
Margaret, born March 22, 1736 ; John Muirhead in Shots
parish, his daughter Elizabeth, born February 14, 1736 ;
Robert Selkirk in Old Munkland, his daughter Janet, born
March 2, 1736.

At Braehead, May 9, 1736, on Sabbath after sermon, were
baptized, David Turnbule in Blantyre, his son James,
born April 1, 1736 ; John Smith in Glasfoord parish his
son James, born May 1, 1736.

At Braehead, May 16, 1736, being Sabbath, after sermon, John
Anderson in Old Munkland parish his son John, born
April 15, 1736, was baptized.

At Braehead, May 23, 1736, on Sabbath, after sermon, John Burnlee in Evandale parish his daughter Jean, born April 10, 1736; John Gowans in Torphichen parish his daughter Margaret, born March 10, 1736; were baptized.

John Carmichal in Douglas parish his son James, born March 12, 1736, and baptized after lecture, at the Tofts, May 28, 1736.

At Mountherick, May 30, 1736, on Sabbath, after sermon, George Porteus in Crafoordjohn parish his daughter Katharine, born March 21, 1736; John Lambie in New Cumlock his daughter Jean, born April 7, 1736; Jo: Robson in Glencairn his son John, born March 31, 1736; James Hair in Kirkconel his daughter Jean, 5 months old; William Clark in Carsfairn his daughter Margaret, born July 1, 1735; Jo: Barber in Glencairn his daughter Jean, born December 20, 1735; were all baptized.

At Braehead, June 13, 1736, on Sabbath, after sermon, John Alexander in Barony parish his son Joseph, born February 10, 1736; James Laurie in Carlucke parish his son Gavin, born April 16, 1736; were baptized.

At Cold-Wakning, June 15, 1736, after lecture, week-day, Robert Hamilton in Evandale his daughter Isobel, 15 weeks old, baptized.

At Mains of Loudon, June 16, 1736, on a week-day, after lecture, William Woodburn in Kilmarnock parish his daughter Mary, born February 3, 1736; Peter Orr in Finnick parish his daughter Agnes, born February 23, 1736; Peter Orr in the same parish his son John, born May 25, 1736; Thomas Boid in Kilmarnock parish his daughter Jean, born December . . . 1735; George Mair in New Milns parish his daughter Jonet, born January 26, 1736; George Hunter in Gaastoun parish his son Robert, born May 10, 1736; all baptized.

At Loanhead, August 4, 1736, after lecture, on a week-day, James Rankin, junior, in the parish of Laswade, had 3 children baptized by the Rev. Mr. John M'Millan :— James, born . . . . . . ; William, born August 2, 1734; Helen, born June . . ., 1736.

At Pentland, August 5, 1736, on a week-day, after sermon, Walter Vetch in Ecfoord, his son James, born November 14, 1733; his daughter Margaret, born November 11, 1735; Robert Fleeming *ibidem*, his sons, James, born September 7, 1734; Robert, born July 5, 1736; James Thomson in Fala parish, his son Thomas, born May 15, 1736; Thomas Wier in Edinburgh, his son Alexander, born November 18, 1735; Alexander Smellie in West Kirk parish of Edinburgh, son John, born June 17, 1736; all baptized by the Rev. Mr. John M'Millan.

At Leathshead, August 6, 1736, after lecture, on a week-day,

Thomas Clarkson in Ratha parish, his son John, born August 6, 1736.

At Tafts near Douglas, July 12, 1736, on a week-day, after lecture, John Ingles in Douglas parish his son Alexander, born June 23, 1736, was baptized.

At Monherick, July 13, 1736, on a week-day, after lecture, baptized William Brown in Craaford parish his son David, born July 8, 1736; William Dixson in Crafordjohn parish his son Thomas, born June 5, 1736.

At Braehead, August 15, 1736, on Sabbath, after sermon, Patrick Robison in Lochwhenoch parish his son Thomas, born July 19, 1736; Lodovick Hill in New Monkland parish his daughter Janet, born August 8, 1736; baptized.

At Braehead, August 22, 1736, on the Sabbath, after sermon (text, Gal. 2. 20, being the last sermon on that text), Hugh Marr in Old parish of Cumlock his daughter Bessie, born July 9, 1736.

At Braehead, August 29, 1736, on the Sabbath, after sermon, William Muckle in parish of Loudon, his son Thomas, born July 28, 1736, was baptized.

At Breahead, September 12, 1736, on the Sabbath after sermon, James Hamilton in Hamilton parish his son James, born August 23, 1736, baptized.

Ibidem, September 14, 1736, being a week-day, after lecture, James Lang in Hamilton his daughter Janet, born August 16, 1736, was baptized.

At Braehead, September 19, 1736, on Sabbath, after sermon, the S[olemn?] L[eague?] being read after:—John Din in parish of Mauchline his daughter Jean, born June 24, 1736; Andrew Smart in Molinside parish, his son Archibald, about a quarter old; baptized.

At Braehead, September 26, 1736, being Sabbath, after sermon, baptized, George Brown in Dalgain parish his son John, born August 12, 1736; James Patterson in Lasmehago parish, his son John, born May 12, 1736, his widow holding up and engaging for the child, himself being dead the summer before.

At Braehead, October 3, 1736, on the Sabbath, after sermon, James Hay in parish of Cumbernauld his son Joseph, born August 20, 1736, was baptized.

At Braehead, October 10, 1736, on Sabbath, after sermon, Samuel Dalziel in Kirconnel parish his son Gavin, born August 27, 1736, was baptized.

At Braehead, October 17, 1736, after sermon, on the Sabbath, James Grahame in parish of Sanquair his son Robert, born July 13, 1736; John Hunter in the same parish his daughter Agnes, born June 2, 1736; were baptized.

At Braehead, October 24, 1736, on Sabbath, after sermon, John Selkirk in parish of New Monkland his daughter Margaret, born September 15, 1736, was baptized.

At Braehead, January 2, 1737, on the Sabbath, after sermon; Mathew Turnbul in parish of Blantyre his daughter Jonet, born November 8, 1736, was baptized.

At Braehead, February 20, 1737, on the Sabbath, after lecture; Jo: Selkirk in parish of Shots, his son Robert, born December 1st, 1736.

Ibid., February 27, 1737, on Sabbath, after sermon; James Hutcheson in Glasgow his daughter Martha, born March 14, 1736.

At Braehead, March 6, 1737, on Sabbath, after sermon, John Jamison in Evandale his daughter Agnes, born December 12, 1736, was baptized.

At Braehead, March 13, 1737, on the Sabbath, after sermon, James Dunlop in Dalcerf parish, his son Gavin, born February 28, 1737, was baptized.

At Bogton, March 17, 1737, after lecture, week-day, Robert Tod in Glasgow, his son John, born January 22d, 1737; James Gourlie in Old Monkland his daughter Jean, born November 9, 1736; Alexander Gairner in Kilmacolm parish his son Alexander, born February 17, 1737; were baptized.

At Braehead, April 10, 1737, after sermon, being Sabbath, John Paul in Loudon parish his daughter Elizabeth, born August 29, 1736; James Dobie in Carluke parish, his son Robert, born November 15, 1736.

At Greenfoot (*me absente*), April 20, 1737, on a week-day after lecture, John Niven in   his daughter Elizabeth, aged 6 weeks; John Paterson in   his son John, aged 5 months; Andrew Cameron in   his daughter Helen, aged 6 months; James Lambie in New-Milns parish his daughter Agnes, born December 1736; William Smith in Killbride parish his son John, aged 6 weeks; James Hamilton in New Milns parish, his son Robert, aged 15 days; were all baptized.

At Braehead, April 24, 1737, on the Sabath, after sermon, David Mathison in the parish of Markins, his son Robert, born October 12, 1736.

At Provin Miln near Glasgow, April 27, 1737, being a week-day, after lecture, William Ralston in Calder parish his daughter Elizabeth; John Gourly in the same parish his son John, born   ; were baptized.

At Drumclog, April 21, 1737, after lecture, was baptized by the Rev. Mr. M'Millan, Michael Cochran in Evandale parish his son Alexander, born March 15, 1737.

At Braehead, May 1, 1737, on the Sabbath, after sermon, John Lang in Cambusnethen parish his son William, born January 12, 1737, was baptized.

At Braehead, May 8, 1737, on Sabbath, after sermon, Andrew Stiel in Hamilton his son James, born March 5, 1737, was baptized.

At Moor-mealing, May 11, 1737, on a week-day, after examination, John Reid in Shots parish his daughter Elizabeth, born April 7, 1737, was baptized.

At Braehead, May 22, 1737, on Sabath, after sermon, Alexander Patterson in Carnwath parish his son Alexander, born February 14, 1737 ; James Smith in Glasfoord parish his daughter Helen, born April 21, 1737 ; were baptized.

At Mountherick near Crawfurdjohn, May 29, 1737, after sermon, were baptized, Archbald Gaa in Muirkirk his daughter Marion, aged about 14 years, taking on the vows herself after examination ; Marion Glendoning in Sanquair her daughter Jean, born May 2, 1737 ; William Cook in Sanquair parish his daughter Grizel, born August 2, 1736 ; William Thoreburn in Sanquair parish his daughter Jean, March 30, 1737 ; John Sampson in Kirkonel parish his son John, born April 10, 1737 ; William Howetson in Crafoord parish his daughter Margaret, born February 28, 1737 ; Ninion Stiel in Kirkonel parish his son Samuel, October 28, 1736 ; William Scot in Roberton parish his son George, born October 1736 ; William Sampson in Douglas his daughter Jean, born September 4, 1736 ; William Atken in Morton parish his daughter Marion, born October 26, 1736 ; William Brown in Kirkonel parish his daughter Christian, born January 4, 1737 ; John Smith in Glencairn parish his son John, born February 5, 1737 ; John Cotes in the parish of Kilpatrick Durham his daughter Mary, born March 19, 1737.

At Braehead, June 5, 1737, on Sabath, after sermon, were baptized John Dobie in Cambusnethan parish his son John, born April 24, 1737 ; James Lang (not the taylor) in Hamilton parish (in Atinton) his son James, born May 2, 1737 ; Daniel Hamilton in Glasfoord parish his daughter Jean.

At Braehead, June 12, 1737, on Sabath, after sermon, were baptized, John Russel in Hamilton his son John, born May 21, 1737 ; Adam Brown in Gaaston his daughter Isobel, aged 9 months.

At Braehead, July 10, 1737, on the Sabbath, after sermon, were baptized, Alexander Fleeming in Collington parish his daughter Jean, March 23, 1737 ; Jo: Pillens in Carstairs parish his son John, born May 23, 1737 ; William Lagan in Bonnel parish his son Robert, born November 1736.

At   near Glasgow, July 14, 1737, on a week-day after lecture, was baptized, James Whitelaw in Calton of Glasgow, Barrony parish, his son William ; born May 31, 1737.

At Braehead, August 7, 1737, on the Sabbath evening after lecture, were baptized, Richard Jackson and Margaret

Forbes in Kilmarnock, their daughter Margaret, born June 25, 1734; their son Boid, born February 1737.

At Braehead, August 21, 1737, on Sabbath, after sermon, Robert Scot and Janet Dalziel in Dalcerf parish their daughter Katharine, born July 31ˢᵗ, 1737, was baptized.

At Braehead, September 4, 1737, on Sabbath, after sermon, James Roger in Shots parish his son Alexander, aged 5 weeks, was baptized.

At Braehead, October 25, 1737, on a week-day, after lecture, James Turnbull and Bethea Nilson their daughter Bethea, born October 6, 1737; and William Turnbull, both in the parish of Blantyre, his son Joseph, born August 31, 1737; were baptized.

At Tafts, October 28, 1737, on a week-day, after lecture, Jo: Ingles in Douglas parish, his daughter Isobel, born September 20, 1737.

At Crafurdjohn, October 30, 1737, on Sabbath, after sermon, Edward Blackstock in Lamington parish his daughter Jean, aged 15 weeks; John Gaa in Douglas parish his son Archbald, aged 2 weeks; Thomas Reid in Crafoord parish his daughter Anna, born October 21, 1737.

Ibid., 31 October, 1737, after lecture, Thomas French in Crafurdjohn parish his son Adam, born October 25, 1737; David French in the same parish his son David, born August 2, 1737; were all baptized.

At Braehead, November 6, 1737, on the Sabath, after sermon, William Gemble in Finnick parish his son William, aged 6 weeks; Jo: Robertson in Hamilton parish his daughter Rebeccah, aged 6 or 8 weeks; were baptized.

At Braehead, December 11, 1737, on Sabbath after sermon, James Lang, younger, in Hamilton, his son James, born October 28, 1737, was baptised.

At Longmuir in Old Monkland parish, January 17, 1738, on a week-day, after lecture, were baptised :—Jo: Anderson in Old Munkland parish his daughter Margaret, aged 3 weeks; Hugh Miller in Barrony parish of Glasgow his son Hugh, 3 months; Robert Ingles in Barrony parish of Glasgow his son Robert, 2 months.

About a mile distant from the said place, same day, after lecture, was baptised, James Gourly in the said parish his son John.

At Airdray, January 18, 1738, after lecture, was baptised James Gardiner in New Munkland parish his daughter Janet.

At Braehead, January 22, 1738, on Sabbath after sermon, John Borland in the parish of Loudon his daughter Grizel, born September 21, 1737; William Mickle in the same parish his son James, born December 5, 1737, were baptised.

At Braehead, January 29, 1738, on the Sabbath after sermon,
James Beg in Muirkirk parish, his daughter Elizabeth, aged
7 weeks, was baptized.

At Dykehead, February 23, 1738, after lecture, being a week-
day, John Watt in Hamilton parish his daughter Jean,
born February 3, 1738, was baptized.

At Braehead, March 12, 1738, on the Sabbath after sermon,
Brice Frame in Carluke parish his son James, born
January 21, 1738, was baptized.

At Braehead, April 2ᵈ, 1738, on the Sabbath after sermon,
John Raining in Preston-Pans his daughter Jean, born
September 3, 1724, and his son John, born October 9,
1729, were baptized.

At Muirmealing, April 24, 1738, on a week-day, after
examination, were baptized, John Gowans in Torphichan
parish his son William, aged 6 weeks; John Hill in Shots
parish his son James, aged   .

At   near Glasgow, April 27, 1738, on a week-day
after lecture, was baptized, John Alexander in Barrony
parish his son Josias, aged 2 weeks.

At Blantyre, April 29, 1738, on a week-day after lecture, were
baptized David Turnbul in Blantyre his   ;
James Gourlay in Old Munkland parish his son James,
born March 24, 1738.

At Braehead, April 30, 1738, on Sabbath after sermon was
baptized, Robert Turnbull in New Munckland parish his
daughter Jean, born February 20, 1738.

At West Forth, May 14, 1738, on Sabbath after sermon, James
Hasty in Laswade parish his daughter Margaret, born
August 7, 1737; Alexander Smellie in West Kirk parish
of Edinburgh his son William, born January 10, 1738;
were baptized.

At Braehead, May 21, 1738, on Sabbath after sermon, John
Young in Kilbride parish his daughter Margaret, born
April 21, 1738; Alexander Hamilton in Gaaston parish
his daughter Mary, born March 7, 1738; James Brouning
in Gaaston parish his daughter Martha, born February 2,
1738; were baptized.

At Mountherick, May 28, 1738, on Sabbath after sermon, were
baptized, William M'Whirie in Tindren parish his son
James, born May 31, 1737; John M'Ceur in Kirkpatrick
his daughter Jonet, aged 9 months; Thomas Moffat in
Crafoordjohn parish his daughter Elizabeth, born November 15, 1737; Thomas Brown in Crafoord parish his
daughter Jean, aged 6 weeks; John Grier in Glencairn
parish his son Samuel, [born] March 2, 1738; William
Shields in Sanquair parish his son Thomas, January 20,
1738; James Mathison in Balmaclelan his daughter Jean,
February 22, 1738; Samuel Dalziel in Kirkconel his son

William, March 17, 1738; James Hair in Kirkconel his son Robert, aged 3 weeks; Archibald Edgar in Crafoord parish his daughter Margaret, November 19, 1737; Adam Blakclay in Crafoordjohn his daughter Jean, April 22, 1738; John Young in Crafoordjohn his son David, February 14, 1738; Adam M'Calsey in Muirkirk his son Agnes, aged six weeks; William Shanklay in Sanquair parish his son George, aged 6 months; James Grahame in Sanquair parish his daughter Agnes, March 9, 1738; Jo: March in Crafoord his daughter Barbary, February 21, 1738.

At Crafoordjohn, May 30, 1738, after lecture were baptized, James Williamson in Kirkconel his son Peter, born October 2, 1735, and also his daughter Anna, February 20, 1738.

At Tafts in Douglass parish, June 21, 1738, after lecture was baptized, William Brown in Crafoord parish his daughter Margaret, born June 11, 1738.

At Braehead, July 2, 1738, was baptized on Sabbath after sermon, James Hamilton in Hamilton parish his son Thomas, born June, 9, 1738.

At Braehead, July 16, 1738, was baptized on the Sabbath after sermon, George Hunter in Gaaston parish his daughter Agnes, born May 18, 1738.

At Braehead, July 23, 1738, was baptized on Sabbath after sermon, James Craig in Srevan parish his daughter Jean, born May 30, 1738.

At Braehead, August 6, 1738, on Sabbath after sermon, Thomas Clarkson in Kirknewton parish his son Thomas, aged 7 weeks, was baptized.

At Braehead, August 13, 1738, on Sabbath after sermon, baptized :—James Dunlop in Dalcerf his son John, aged 7 weeks; John Smith in Glasfoord parish his son John, born August 2, 1738; Robert Inglis in Douglas parish his daughter Grizel, born July 8, 1738; Daniel Hamilton in Glasfoord parish his daughter Jannet, aged 3 weeks.

At Braehead, September 3, 1738, on Sabbath after sermon was baptized, William Martin in Shots parish his son John, aged 5 weeks.

At Braehead, September 5, 1738, on a week-day, after lecture, was baptized, James Hamilton in Hamilton his son John, born August 18, 1738.

At Braehead, October 1, 1738, on Sabbath after sermon, was baptized, James Mitchel in Old Cumnuck parish his son James, born August 15, 1738.

At Peat-Pots, October 22, 1738, on Sabbath after sermon, were baptized, William Thomson in Shots parish his daughter Jean, born September 15, 1738; John Muirhead in the same parish his son James, born May 31, 1738.

At Braehead, October 29, 1738, on Sabbath after sermon, was baptized, James Coupar in Dalcerf parish his daughter Anna, born September—1738.

At Crafoordjohn, November 5, 1738, on Sabbath after sermon, were baptized :—Jo : Gall in Crafoordjohn his son James, born October 28, 1738 ; Gilbert Watson in Crafoord parish his son Gilbert, born June 8, 1738 ; Robert Marshal in Crafoordjohn his daughter Agnes, born September 8, 1738 ; Robert Craig in Crafordjohn his daughter Jean, born October 8, 1738 ; John Barber in Glencairn his daughter Janet, September 20, 1738.

At Tafts, November 8, 1738, on a week-day after lecture was baptized, James Muir in Douglass his son John, aged 7 weeks.

At Braehead, November 19, 1738, on Sabbath after sermon, were baptized, William Patterson in Cambusnethen parish, his daughter Jean, born October 30, 1738 ; Patrick Robertson in Lochneuch parish, his daughter Jean, born October 22, 1738.

At Breahead, December 5, 1738, on Sabbath after sermon, was baptized, John Burnlee in Evandale, his son James, born October 4, 1738.

At Braehead, March 4, 1739, on Sabbath after sermon, was baptized, Matthew Turnbull in Blantyre parish, his daughter Mary, aged 15 weeks.

At Langmure, March 21, 1739, on a week-day, after lecture, were baptized ; James Whitelaw in Glasgow his son John, aged 2 weeks ; Robert Selkirk in Old Munkland his daughters Margaret and Christian, aged 6 days ; Loudovick Hill in New Munckland his daughter Margaret, aged 3 weeks ; Gavin Black in the same parish his son Gavin, aged 5 weeks.

At Braehead, April 15, 1739, on Sabbath after sermon, was baptized, Ja : Turnbull, younger, in Blantyre parish, his daughter Janet, born February 14, 1739.

At Braehead, April 22, 1739, on Sabbath after sermon was baptized Robert Ingles in Barrony parish of Glasgow his son Robert, born March 27, 1739.

At Law in Carluke parish, April 19, 1739, on a week-day after lecture, was baptized, James Doby in Carluke, his son Daniel, aged   weeks.

At Braehead, May 6, 1739, on Sabbath after sermon was baptized, William Ralton, younger, in Calder parish near Glasgow, his son Alexander, born April 15, 1739.

At Breahead, May 18, 1739, on a week-day after lecture, George Mair in Loudon parish, his son John, born August 9, 1738, was baptized.

At Braehead, May 24, 1739, on a week-day after lecture, was baptized, John Watt in Hamilton parish, his son Archibald, born April 13, 1739.

At Crafoordjohn, May 27, 1739, on Sabbath after sermon, were baptized, Ninian Steil in Kirkonnel parish, his son Archibald, born August 1738; Adam Gall in Sanquair parish, his son John, November 7, 1738; William Cunningham in Kirkpatrick Durham, his son William, December 15, 1738; Patrick Hair in Sanquair parish, his son Ninian, aged   months; William Brown, Kirkonnel parish, his daughter Jean, born March 6, 1739; William Laidlaw in the parish of Line, his daughter Isobel, April 23, 1739; James Widrington in Sanquair parish, his son Edward, December 15, 1738; Jo: Black in Ettrick parish his son Andrew, December 20, 1738.

At Tafts, near Douglass, May 29, on a week-day after lecture, was baptized, Jo: Carmichael in Douglass, his son John, [born] February 7, 1739.

At Braehead, July 1, 1739, were baptized on Sabbath after sermon, Robert Scot, younger, in Dalcerf parish, his son Jo: and daughter Grizel, born June 28, 1739.

At Braehead, July 22, 1739, were baptized on Sabbath after sermon, Jo: Alexander in Barony parish of Glasgow, his daughter Jean, born June 27, 1739; Jo: Selkirk in Shots parish, his son David, born June 23, 1739; Jo: Pillans in Carstairs parish, his son Thomas, aged 6 weeks; James Smith in Glasfoord parish his daughter Margaret, born June 22, 1739.

At Breahead, August 3, 1739, was baptized on Sabbath after sermon, Thomas Henderson, younger, in Middleby parish, his daughter Barbara, born December 1, 1738.

At Breahead, August 12, 1739, were baptized on Sabbath after sermon, Peter Orr in Kilmarnock parish, his son Andrew, aged 5 weeks; James Lang in Hamilton parish, his son John, born July 31, 1739.

At Braehead, September 16, 1739, on Sabbath after sermon were baptized, John Sampson in Kirkconnell, his daughter Janet, born August 9, 1739; John Russel in Hamilton, his son William, born August 22, 1739.

At Braehead, September 23, 1739, on Sabbath after sermon, was baptised, James Hutcheson in Glasgow, his son Robert, born July 27, 1739.

At Braehead, October 7, 1739, on Sabbath after sermon, was baptized William Orr in Kilmarrs parish, his son William, born July 24, 1739.

At Dunseiston, in Shots parish, October 14, 1739, on Sabbath after sermon, were baptized, William Thomson in Shots parish, his son John, born September 16, 1739; Jo: Reid in the same parish, his daughter Marion, born October 11, 1739.

At Forth, October 21, 1739, on Sabbath after sermon, were baptized David Mathison in Markins parish, his son James, born May 1, 1739; Alexander Fleeming in Collington parish, his son Alexander, born August 12, 1739.

At Braehead, October 23, 1739, on a week-day after lecture, was baptized, William Gilrie in Dreghorn parish, his daughter Mary, aged 2 years.

In Munkland parish, October 8, 1739, on a week-day after lecture was baptized, John Anderson in Old Munkland parish, his daughter Janet, aged 3 weeks.

At Braehead, January 27, 1740, on Sabbath after sermon, was baptized, Jackson and Margaret Forbes in Kilmarnock their daughter Margaret, born March 16, 1739.

At Braehead, February 11, 1740, after lecture on a week-day was baptized, William Turnbull in Blantyre parish his son William, born November 4, 1739.

At Braehead, March 23, 1740, after sermon was baptized, John Marshal in Bothwel parish his son Robert, aged 4 months.

Ibidem, March 30, 1740, on Sabbath after sermon, was baptized James Turnbull in Blantyre his daughter Janet, born February 14, 1740.

At Muirmealing, April 13, 1740, were baptized after sermon, Thomas Stiel in Shots parish his daughter Janet, born March 20, 1740; James Japhrie in the same parish his daughter Ann, born March 14, 1740; John Roger in the said parish his daughter Marion, born April 10, 1740.

At Braehead, May 4, 1740, on Sabbath after sermon, John Young his daughter Margaret, January 1, 1740; Thomas Broun his son John, aged 5 weeks; both in Crafoordjohn parish.

At Braehead, May 11, 1740, on Sabbath after sermon baptized, William Brown in Crafoord parish his daughter Katharine, born March 30, 1740; James Scouler in Evandale his daughter Janet, born March 31, 1740; Adam Blakely in Crawfoordjohn parish his daughter Sarah, aged 7 weeks.

At Braehead, May 25, 1740, on Sabbath after sermon was baptized, John Paul in New Milns parish his son James, born May 21, 1740.

At Tafts, May 27, 1740, on a week-day after lecture were baptized, Robert Ingles in Douglas Parish his son John, born May 6, 1740; James Muir in Douglas his daughter Euphan, aged   weeks.

At Crafoordjohn, May 28, 1740, after lecture was baptized, Adam Laidly in Tweedsmuir parish his son William, aged 7 months.

At Braehead, June 15, 1740, after sermon on the Sabbath were baptized, Alexander Smellie in West Kirk parish his daughter Elizabeth, born January , 1740; William

M'Whirr in Tinron parish his daughter Mary, born November 10, 1739; Jo: Barber in Glencairn parish his daughter Anna, born April 1740.

At Braehead, June 22ᵈ, 1740, on Sabbath after sermon was baptized, William Gilrie in Dreghorn parish his daughter Jean, born March 19, 1740.

At Braehead, June 29, 1740, on Sabbath after sermon were baptized, James Hasty in Laswade parish his daughter Helen, born October 17, 1739; James Browning in Glastoun parish his son John, born May 5, 1740; William Logan in Kilmaronock parish his son Alexander, aged 6 months.

At Braehead, July 13, 1740, on Sabbath after sermon was baptized, Archibald Edgar in Crafoord parish his son Archibald, born February 20, 1740.

Near Glasgow, June 3, 1740, Hugh Miller in Barrony parish his

At Braehead, July 27, 1740, on Sabbath after sermon was baptized, William Fullerton in Balmagie parish his daughter Janet, born February 20, 1740.

At Braehead, August 28, 1740, on a week-day after lecture were baptized, David Turnbule in Blantyre parish his son David, born August 1, 1740; James Hamilton in Hamilton his son Alexander, born August 8, 1740.

At Braehead, October 19, 1740, on Sabbath after sermon was baptized, Jo: Grieve in Middleby parish his son Thomas, born September 13, 1740.

At Drumclog, October 22, 1740, on a week-day after lecture was baptized, Jo: Jamison in Evandale parish his son Andrew, born July 3, 1740.

At Braehead, October 30, on a week-day after lecture was baptized James Smith in Glasfoord parish his son John, born September 3, 1740.

At Braehead, December 21, 1740, on Sabbath after sermon was baptized, Gavin Neilson in West Calder parish his son Thomas, born November 5, 1740.

At Braehead, February 15, 1740, on Sabbath after sermon was baptized, Jo: Ingles in Douglass parish his son William, born October 31, 1740.

At Braehead, March 29, 1741, on Sabbath after sermon was baptized, Mathew Turnbull in Blantyre parish his daughter Marion.

At Mountherick, May 6, 1741, on a week-day after lecture were baptized, David Trench in Crafurdjohn, his daughter Sarah, born April 4, 1741; Thomas Trench *ibidem* his son Thomas, born 20 of November 1740; Thomas Mathison in   his daughter Ester, born June 28, 1740; Elizabeth Gibson in   her daughter Jean, 29 of June 1740.

Ibidem, May 7, 1741, on a week-day after sermon were

baptized, Jo: March in Crawfurd parish his son John, born September 23, 1740; Jo: Robertson in the parish of Killpatrick-Durham his daughter Jean, July 2, 1740; Robert Cunninghame *ibidem* his daughter Jean, August 26, 1740; Jo: Grier in Glencairn parish his daughter Janet, born June 22, 1740; Peter Raining in Tinwald parish his son John, January 14, 1741; William Laidlaw in Line parish his daughter Helen, January 25, 1741; Jo: Blake in Etrick parish his daughter Mary, aged 3 months; Alexander Hislop in the parish of Askine, Margaret, aged 15 months.

At Tafts, May 8, 1741, was baptized on a week-day after lecture, Jo: Carmichael in Douglass his

At Braehead, May 17, 1741, was baptized on Sabbath after sermon, John Anderson in Old Munkland his daughter Janet, born April 8, 1741.

At Braehead, May 28, 1741, on a week-day after lecture was baptized, Adam Mienzies of Troloss in Crawfurd parish his son George, born February 14, 1741.

At Braehead, May 31, 1741, on Sabbath after sermon were baptized, Jo: Alexander in Barrony parish his daughter Elizabeth, born January 4, 1741; Jo: Young in Kilbride parish his son John, aged 6 weeks.

At Braehead, June 7, 1741, on Sabbath after sermon was baptized, William Ralston in Calder parish his daughter Lillias, born April 28, 1741.

At Braehead, July 19, 1741, on Sabbath after sermon were baptized, John Selkirk in Old Munkland parish his son, born May 31, 1741; John Dobie in Lesmahagow parish his son   , born May 23, 1741.

At Braehead, July 26, 1741, on Sabbath after sermon were baptized, John Hill in Shots parish his son George, born February 4, 1741; Robert Selkirk in Old Munkland parish his son Robert, born May 29, 1741.

At Braehead, August 2, 1741, on Sabbath after sermon were baptized, Thomas Clarkson in Kirknewton parish his daughter Elizabeth, born April 12, 1741; David Mathison in the parish of Bingry his daughter Elizabeth, born May 1741.

At Redmire, August 16, 1741, on Sabbath after sermon was baptized, John Hamilton in Cambusnethen parish his daughter Elizabeth, born June 14, 1741.

At Braehead, March 7, 1742, on Sabbath after sermon were baptized, James Craig and Elizabeth Jamison in Evandale parish his daughter Janet, born January 6, 1742; John Red in Shots parish his daughter Margaret, born December 11, 1741.

At Braehead, April 4, 1742, on Sabbath after sermon was baptized, Thomas Telfer in Cambusnethen parish his daughter Jean, aged 15 years.

At Braehead, April 25, 1742, on Sabbath after lecture was
baptized, James Muir in Douglass his daughter Marion,
born March 25, 1742.

At Braehead, May 2, 1742, on Sabbath after lecture were
baptized, William Brown in Crawfurd parish his daughter
Mary, born November 25, 1741; Thomas Stiel in Shots
parish his daughter Jean, born March 25, 1742; William
Thomson in Shots parish his son James, born
March 31, 1742; John Roger in Shots parish his son James,
born February 28, 1742.

At Braehead, May 18, 1742, on a week-day after lecture was
baptized, Jackson and Margaret Forbes in Bathgate
parish their son Robert, born August 31, 1741.

At Braehead, May 23, 1742, on Sabbath after sermon was
baptized, William Brown in Kirkonel parish his son
William, born August 4, 1741.

At Braehead, May 30, 1742, on Sabbath after sermon were
baptized, Thomas Henderson younger in Middleby
parish his son Thomas, born December 29, 1741; Jo:
Young in Sanquair parish his daughter Jean, born
January 11, 1742; Thomas Broun in Crawfordjohn parish
his daughter Mary, born March 4, 1742; James Trench
in Crawfordjohn parish his daughter Janet, born May 1,
1742; Adam Blakely in the same parish his son William,
aged 5 weeks.

At Braehead, June 6, 1742, on Sabbath after sermon was
baptized, Hugh Thomson in Shots parish his son John,
born May 7, 1742.

At Braehead, June 13, 1742, on Sabbath after sermon was
baptized, John Allan in Cambusnethen parish his daughter
Marion, born May 14, 1742.

At Braehead, June 27, 1742, on Sabbath after sermon were
baptized, Matthew Turnbul in Blantyre parish his son
James, born April 18, 1742; William Logan in Bonnel
parish his son John, aged 7 months.

At West Forth, July 4, 1742, on Sabbath after sermon was
baptized, Daniel Sympson in Carnwath parish his son
Daniel, born June 6, 1742.

At Braehead, July 15, 1742, on a week-day after lecture was
baptized, James Lang, younger in Hamilton, his daughter
Anna, born June 8, 1742.

At Braehead, July 25, 1742, on Sabbath after sermon was
baptized, Mary Love, widow of Alexander Gardiner in
Newport, Glasgow, their son David, born June 21,
1742.

At Braehead, August 8, 1742, on Sabbath after sermon were
baptized, Thomas Johnston in Eskdale his son William,
and his daughter Margaret, aged 10 months.

At Braehead, September 12, 1742, on Sabbath after sermon

was baptized, John M'Farlin in Glasgow his son John, born August 3, 1742.

At Braehead, September 26, 1742, on Sabbath after sermon were baptized, William Orr in Kilmawrs parish his daughter Jean, born August 11, 1742; Robert Keneday in Lesmahago parish, his daughter Mary, born September 18, 1742.

At Hamilton, November 16, 1742, on a week day after lecture was baptized, James Turnbul and Bethea Neilson in Blantyre, their daughter Marion, born September 29, 1742.

At Braehead, December 26, 1742, on Sabbath after sermon was baptized, Peter Orr in Kilmarnock parish his son Peter, aged 12 weeks.

At Braehead, December 30, 1742, on a week-day after lecture was baptized, Thomas Ried in Crawfoord parish his son Charles, born August 25, 1742.

At Langmuir, April 13, 1743, on a week-day after lecture were baptized, John Anderson in Old Munkland parish his son William, aged 7 weeks; John Alexander in Barrony parish his son Moses; John Selkirk in Old Munkland his daughter Janet, aged 8 days.

At Braehead, May 15, 1743, on Sabbath after sermon were baptized, James Smith in Hamilton parish his daughter Katherine, aged three weeks; William Smith in Hamilton parish his son John, aged five weeks.

At Braehead, May 22, 1743, on Sabbath after sermon was baptized, James Craig, shoemaker in Evandale, his daughter Janet, born February 13, 1743.

At Mountherick, May 29, 1743, after lecture was baptized, William Brown in Kirkonell parish his son Peter, born May 13, 1743.

At Tafts, May 31, 1743, after lecture was baptized, John Carmichal in Douglass parish his son George.

At Braehead, June 19, 1743, after sermon was baptized on Sabbath, William Ralton in Calder parish his daughter Margaret, born April 20, 1743.

At Braehead, July 7, 1743, on a week-day after lecture was baptized, James Hamilton in Hamilton his daughter Margaret, born March 19, 1743.

Braehead, July 11, 1743, on Sabbath after sermon was baptized, Robert Anderson in New Monkland parish his son John, aged 15 weeks.

Braehead, July 31, 1743, on Sabbath after sermon were baptized Jo: Selkirk in Glasgow, his son John aged 5 weeks; Gavin Nielson in Cambusnethen parish his son James.

Braehead, August 7, 1743, on Sabbath after sermon was baptized, Robert Ingles in Douglass parish his son Robert, born June 30, 1743.

Braehead, August 28, 1743, on Sabbath after sermon was baptized, Ludovick Hill in New Monkland parish his son Loudovick, born July 15, 1743.

Braehead, October 2, 1743, on Sabbath after sermon, baptized by Mr. Nairn, David Trench in Crawfoordjohn parish his daughter Marion, aged 4 weeks.

Braehead, October 9, 1743, on Sabbath after sermon baptized by Mr. M'Millan, David Turnbull in Blantyre parish his daughter Jean, aged 4 weeks; John Montgumry in Eglesim parish his son Joseph, aged 5 weeks; John Whitlaw in Lesmahago parish his son John, aged 15 days.

Braehead, November 20, 1743, on Sabbath after sermon, baptized by Mr. M'Millan, John Young in Killbride parish his daughter Jean, aged 4 weeks.

Braehead, November 25, 1743, on Sabbath after sermon baptized by Mr. M'Millan, John Watt in Hamilton parish his daughter Janet, born October 30, 1743.

Braehead, January 1, 1744, on Sabbath after sermon was baptized by Mr. M'Millan, Jo: Hamilton in Cambusnethen parish his daughter Agness, born November 25, 1743.

Braehead, January 22, 1744, on Sabbath after sermon baptized by the Rev. Mr. M'Millan, William Thomson in Shots parish his daughter Mary, born December 9, 1743.

Braehead, February 12, 1744, on Sabbath after sermon baptized by Mr. Nairn, James Craig in Evandale his son Matthew, born January 27, 1744.

Braehead, March 11, 1744, on Sabbath after sermon baptized by Mr. M'Millan, Robert Kennedey in Leshmahego parish his daughter Jean, born February 19, 1744.

Braehead, April 1, 1744, on Sabbath after sermon was baptized by Mr. M'Millan, Jo: Roger in Shots parish his son William, born March 3, 1744.

Braehead, April 22, 1744, on Sabbath after sermon was baptized by the Rev. Mr. M'Millan, Robert Hamilton in Evandale parish his son John, born July 23, 1743.

Braehead, May 6, 1744, on Sabbath after sermon was baptized by the Rev. Mr. M'Millan, John Allan in Cambusnethen parish his daughter Janet, born March 24, 1744; Adam Gaa in Lesmahego parish his daughter Marion, born September 29, 1743.

Braehead, May 13, 1744, on Sabbath after sermon was baptized by Mr. M'Millan, Hugh Thomson in Shots parish his son John, born April 8, 1744.

Braehead, May 27, 1744, on Sabbath after sermon was baptized by Mr. Nairn, John Dobie, younger, in Shots parish his daughter Mary, born March 26, 1744.

Braehead, June 27, 1744, on a week-day after lecture was

baptized by Mr. Nairn, Thomas Duncan in Barrony parish his daughter Agnes, born April 1, 1744.

Brae Head, July 8, 1744, on Sabbath was baptised by the Rev. Mr. M'Millan, Joseph Millar in New Monkland parish his daughter Elisabeth, born May 1, 1744.

Brae-Head, July 10, 1744, after lecture was baptised by the Rev. Mr. M'Millan, William Trumbel in Blantar parish his son John, born May 22, 1744.

Brae-Head, July 15, 1744, on Sabbath after sermon was baptised by the Rev. Mr. M'Millan, John Hill in Shots parish his daughter Agnes, born June 17, 1744.

Brae-Head, July 22, 1744, on Sabbath after sermon was baptised by the Rev. Mr. M'Millan, Adam Pedan in Kilbraid parish his son William, born July 3; also Thomas Stiel in Shots parish his son James, born June 13, 1744.

At Couter-Park, July 28, 1744, on a week-day after sermon was baptized by the Rev. Mr. Nairn, Thomas Anderson in Biggar his daughter Elspet, born

At Crawfurdjohn, July 29, 1744, on Sabbath after sermon were baptised by the Rev. Mr. Nairn, James Muir in Douglass his son James, aged 8 weeks; James French in Crawfurdjohn parish his son Adam, born May 30, 1744.

At Crawfurdjohn, July 30, 1744, on a week-day after sermon by Mr. Marshal, probationer, was baptized by the Rev. Mr. Nairn, minister of the Gospel, Thomas Broun in Crawfurdjohn parish his daughter Janet, born

At Tafts near Douglass, July 31, 1744, after sermon was baptised by the Rev. Mr. Nairn, John Inglis in Douglass parish his daughter Jean, born June 1, 1744.

At Braehead, Agust 12, on Sabbath was baptised (after sermon) by the Rev. Mr. M'Millan, William Martin in Shots parish his daughter Mary, born June 9th.

Braehead, September 9, 1744, on Sabbath after sermon was baptized by the Rev. Mr. M'Millan, Jo: Pillans in Carnwath parish his daughter Agness, born August 29, 1744.

Braehead, September 23, 1744, on Sabbath after sermon was baptized by the Rev. Mr. M'Millan, James Turnbul, younger, in Blantyre parish, his son Alexander, born August 7, 1744.

Braehead, October 29, 1744, on Munday after serman were baptised by Mr. Nairn, Gavin Rowat in Stonehouse his 3 sons, Gavin, Thomas, and James.

Braehead, March 8, 1747, on Saboth after sermon was baptized by the Rev. Mr. M'Millan, Jo: Allan in Cambusnethen parish his daughter Jean, born December 13, 1746.

Braehead, May 3ᵈ, 1747, on Saboth after sermon was baptized by the Rev. Mr. M'Millan, Thomas Prentice in Carnwath parish his daughter Jonet born January 6, 1747.

Braehead, May 21, 1747, on Thursday after lecture was baptized by the Rev. Mr. M'Millan, James Hamilton in Hamiltown his daughter Janet, born April 11, 1747.

Greenfoot, June 10, 1747, on Saboth after sermon was baptized by the Rev. Mr. Marshall, William Ore his son Robert, born the 9th of June 1747.

Greenfoot, June 29, 1747, on Saboth after sermon was baptized by the Rev. Mr. Marshall, Peter Ore his daughter Jonet, born March 18, 1747.

At Shank near Arn[i]s[ton], October 5, 1747, on Saboth after sermon was baptized by the Rev. Mr. Marshall, William Black his daughter Janet, born near the beginning of September 1747.

Greenfoot, · September 6, 1747, on Saboth after sermon was baptized by the Rev. Mr Cuth : James Huie his daughter Jullie, in Loudon parish.

Craighead, April 3ᵈ, 1745, on Saboth after sermon, was baptized by the Rev. Mr. Alexander Marshall, George Shaw his daughter Mary, in Kilmadock parish, aged six weeks.

Ab eodem, November 22, 1747, was baptized the same George Shaw in the same parish his daughter Grizel, born the 6th of November 1747.

Att Drumclog, February 29, 1748, after sermon was baptized by the Rev. Mr. Alexander Marshal, Jo : Carnduff in the parish of Evandale his daughter Mary, aged one day.

Att Braehead, Aprill 3, 1748, on Sabbath after sermon was baptized, by the Rev. Mr. Jo : Cuth : Thomas Steel his son John, living in the parish of Shots, born February 18, 1748.

Att Braehead, May 10, 1748, on Wednesday after lecture was baptized by the Rev. Mr. Jo : M'Millan, Robert Kennedy his son Robert, living in the parish of Lesmahago, born Aprill 25, 1748.

Att Braehead, January 14, 1748, on Sabboth after sermon was baptized by the Rev. Mr. Alexander Marshall, William Rodger his son John, in the parish of Old Munckland, born the 21 of November 1747.

Att Reedmire, May 15, 1748, was baptized by the Rev. Mr. Alexander Marshal on Sabbath after sermon, John Wilson in parish of Shots his son William, born the 26 of Apprill 1748; Thomas Mure his daughter Ann, in the same parish born 11 of February 1748, his wife Marry Waddel being sponsor.

Att Braehead, June 11th, 1748, on a week-day after lecture was baptized by the Rev. Mr. Jo : M'Millan, James Turnbull in the parish of Blanter his son William, born Aprill 11, 1748.

Att Flemington, October 17, 1748, was baptized by the Rev.

5

Mr. Alexander Marshall after lecture, Ja : Murhead in the parish of Dalziel, his daughter Elizabeth, born the 14 of October 1748.

Att Henderston, January 20, 1749, was baptized by the Rev. Mr. Alexander Marshall after lecture, Alexander Thomson his son Robert, in the parish of Pasly, aged two weeks.

Att Braehead, Aprill 19, 1749, were baptized by the Rev. Mr. Jo : M'Millan after lecture, William Smith his son William in the parish of Hamilton, born January 7, 1749; David Turnbull in the parish of Blanter his son Jo: born February 6, 1749; Edom Peden in the same parish his daughter born Aprill 2, 1749.

John Pillans in the parish of Carstairs had a daughter baptized called Marion, at Bothwel after lectur the 20 of October, 1749.

John Wilson in Hifflet had a daughter born on the eleventh of February 1751 and baptized the 7th of March after lectur, by Mr. John M'Millan, minister, called Margaret.

The following entries form a separate section in the Register, and consist of Marriages, all of which were celebrated by the Rev. John M'Millan except where otherwise stated; the period embraced being 1735 to 1744 :—

John Jamison and Jannet Mitchel, both in the parish of Evandale, having produced sufficient testimonials, were proclaimed, and upon the 30th day of October 1735 were married at Braehead by the Rev. Mr. John M'Millan.

David Selkirk and Mary Smelie, both in Old Munkland parish being proclaimed on production of sufficient testimonials, were married at Braehead, 13th November 1735.

James Urie in the parish of Govan and Agnes Sinclair in Glasgow were proclaimed as above and married at Braehead 27th November 1735.

James Beg in the parish of Muirkirk, and Isobel Duncan in Dalgain parish, proclaimed as above and married at Braehead 22^d January 1736.

William Selkirk in New Monkland parish and Jean Marshal in Cumbernald parish, proclaimed as above and married at Braehead 23^d March 1736.

At Braehead, April 23, 1736, John Russel in Hamilton and Margaret Downs in Shots parish, after proclamation upon their producing testimonials, were married.

At Braehead, April 26, 1736, Mr. Alexander Marshal in Kingkardine parish and Anna Christie in Dumblane, after proclamation as above, were married.

At Braehead, April 30, 1736, John Thomson in Torphichen parish and Katharine Salmond in New Munkland parish, and also John Borland in Loudon parish and Janet Hamilton in Gaaston parish, being all attested for and proclaimed, were married.

At Braehead, May 26, 1736, James Hamilton in Glasfoord parish and Jonet Lowrie in Evandale parish, having produced testificates were proclaimed there, and married.

At Crafoordjohn, May 31, 1736, were married :—James Mathison and Mary Cuningham, both in Balmaclelland parish ; Jo : Cotes in Glencairn parish and Nicolas Cunningham in Kilpatrick-Durham parish ; Jo : Charters and Bethia Geddes, both in Balmagie parish ; all after proclamation on producing sufficient testimonials.

At Braehead, June 14, 1736, Gilbert Watson and Margaret Watson in Crafoord parish ; and June 15, John Reid and Agnes Hamilton in Shots parish, were married, after attestation and proclamation.

At Braehead, July 5, 1736, William Jamison and Margaret Smith, both in Glasgow, being attested for and proclaimed, were married.

Att Braehead, July 12, 1736, Thomas Osburn and Janet Spear both in New Cumnock parish, married as above.

At Braehead, October 25, 1736, James Wilson and Jean Orr both in Kilmarrs parish, married as above.

At Braehead, December 16, 1736, Matthew Craig and Marion Aird both in Evandale parish, married as above.

At Braehead, December 27, James Turnbull in Blantyre parish and Bethia Nilson in Cambusnethen parish, married as above.

Ibid., December 29, 1736, John Whitlaw and Mary Thomson both in New Monkland parish, married as above.

At Braehead, April 11, 1737, Alexander Hamilton and Jean Hunter both in Gaaston parish, were married as above.

At Braehead, April 25, 1737, Robert Whyte and Alison Thomson both in Torphichen parish, were married.

At Crawfurdjohn, May 30, 1737, were married, William Ladlaw in the parish of Line and Bethia Linton in Etrick parish, being attested for and proclaimed.

At Braehead, June 13, 1737, John Riddel in Askirk parish and Janet Tait in Wilton parish, married as above.

At Braehead, July 28, 1737, Jo : M'Cowan in Kirkonel parish and Margaret Hamilton in Sanquair parish, married as above.

At Braehead, August 23, 1737, William Thomson and Jean Ried both in Shots parish, married as above.

At Braehead, November 17, 1737, Jo : Richmond in Muirkirk parish and Mary Ker in the parish of New Cumnock, married as above.

At Braehead, November 28, 1737, James Ronald and Elspet Ronald, both in Carnbee parish, married as above.

At Braehead, August 3, 1737, Gabriel Thomson and Margaret Murray in Glasgow, married as above.

At Braehead, March 24, 1738, were married, Walter Touch

and Helen Portous, both in Edinburgh, where they were proclaimed and had sufficient testimonials from the Societies there.

At Braehead, April 26, 1738, were married, John M'Cowan in Kirkonel parish and Janet M'Call in Sanquair parish, after attestation and proclamation.

At Mountherick, May 29, 1738, James Wilson in Currie parish and Marion Lawson in Edinburgh, married as above.

At Crafoordjohn, May 29, 1738, William Boswal and Isobel Robson, both in Glencairn, and Thomas Mickle and Marion Woodburn, both in Loudon, married as above.

At Crafoordjohn, November 6, 1738, Adam Laidlaw in the parish of Line and Margaret Brunton in Tweedsmuir parish, married as above.

At Braehead, November 13, 1738, William Orr in Killmars parish and Jean Brown, in Finnick parish, married as above.

At Braehead, April, 1739, James Scouler and Janet Smith, both in Lesmahegow parish, married as above.

At Braehead, August, 1739, Daniel Kilpatrick and Anna Cassels, both in Lessmahagow, married as above.

At Braehead, April 9, 1739, were married, Adam Menzies in Crawford parish and Jean Williamson in Sanquair parish, after attestation and proclamation.

At Braehead, October 10, 1739, Edward Black and Katherine Clark, both in Sanquair parish, married as above.

At Muirmealing in Shots parish, Gavin Neilson and Margaret Fairlay in Shots parish, married as above.

At Braehead, April 21, 1740, James Hamilton in Gaaston parish and Mary Niven in Loudon parish, married as above.

At Braehead, June 27, 1740, Jo: and Agnes Selkirks, in Old-munkland parish, were married as above.

At Black-Hall, August 11, 1740, John Hamilton and Janet Pettecrue in Cambusnethan parish, married as above.

At Braehead, August 18, 1740, Hugh Thomson and Margaret Clide in Shots parish, married as above.

At Braehead, November 11, 1740, James Craig in parish of Evandale and Elizabeth Jamison in Lowdon parish, married as above.

At Braehead, November 24, 1740, James Burns in Douglas parish and Jean Williamson in Wiston parish, married as above; and Robert Kenedy and Isobel Mack, both in Lesmahago.

Ibidem, December 5, 1740, Jo: Nasmith and Janet Wilson, both in Hamilton parish, were married as above.

At Pentland, September 25, 1740, James M'Neil and Margaret Stoddart, both in Laswade parish, married as above.

At Braehead, December 19, 1740, were married, William Nickle and Jean Brounlee in Shots parish, having been attested for and proclaimed.

At Braehead, February 26, 1741, Jo: Tennant and Mary Galloway, both in Calder parish, married as above.

At Braehead, May 1, 1741, Jo: Blake in Peebles parish and Margaret Henderson in Yaraw, married as above.

At Braehead, May 4, 1741, Jo: Tacket in Carluke parish and Jean Chambers in Shots parish, married as above.

At Mountherick, May 6, 1741, James French and Mary Porteus, both in Crawfoordjohn parish, married as above.

At Braehead, May 26, 1741, John Allan and Janet Morton, both in Dalziel parish, married as above.

At Braehead, October 19, 1741, William Ralton in Calder parish and Jean Plean in Carntilloch, married as above.

At Braehead, March 29, 1742, Hugh Grahame and Helen Vetch, both in Newlands parish, married as above.

At Braehead, April 29, 1742, Jo: Pillans and Katherine Martin both in Carstairs parish, married as above; and next day, James Smith and Anna Lang, both in Hamilton.

At Braehead, June 11, 1742, William Smith and Anna Cuthbert both in the parish of Hamilton, married as above.

At Braehead, July 19, 1742, Charles Umpherston and Helen M'Niel, both in Laswade parish, married as above.

At Braehead, November 13, 1742, Thomas Broun and Margaret Gifford, both in Currie parish, married as above.

At Braehead, March 4, 1743, John Stevenson and Janet Aitken, both in the parish of Hamilton, married as above.

At Braehead, May 26, 1743, after attestation and proclamation were married, Archibald Burns in Hamilton parish and Helen Craig in Dalcerf parish.

At Mountherick, May 30, 1743, John Reecky in Biggar, and Isobel Porteus in Coventon parish, married as above.

At Braehead, July 1, 1743, Thomas Duncan and Giles Nizbet, both in Barrony parish of Glasgow, married as above.

At Braehead, August 19, 1743, Adam Peden and Janet More, both Cambuslang parish, married as above.

At Leadhills, October 4, 1743, Andrew Kennedy and Mary Williamson, both in Crawfoord parish, were married by the Rev. Mr. Nairn, after attestation and proclamation.

At Breahead, December 9, 1743, after attestation and proclamation, John Anderson in Galston parish and Jean Craig in Evandale parish were married by the Rev. Mr. Jo: M'Millan.

At Braehead, December 17, 1743, after attestation and proclamation, Alexander Kirkland and Elizabeth Cuthbertson, both in Kilmarnock parish, were married by the Rev. Mr. Jo: M'Millan.

At Braehead, April 11, 1744, after attestation and proclamation, Andrew Broun and Janet Clyde both in Egglesham parish, were married by the Rev. Mr. Tho: Nairn.

At Braehead, May 28, 1744, James Nielson and Margaret Brounlie, both in the Shots parish, having been attested for and proclaimed, were married by the Rev. Mr. Nairn.

At Loanhead, June 29, 1744, after attestation and proclamation, Robert Hutchison in Tranent parish and Janet M'Niel in Laswade parish, were married by the Rev. Mr. Nairn.

At Braehead, October 22, 1744, after attestation and proclamation, Hugh Pattison and Margaret Tennant, both in Carnwath parish, were married by the Rev. Mr. M'Millan.

At Craford John, February 28, 1707.

An acompt of the destribution of the colection to the poor in the shyres following :—

TIVIOTDALE.—Helen Fish and Margaret Fish	01	10	00
ANANDALE.—Blench Ferguson	00	14	00
NITH.—John Harron	02	00	00
Marion Tait	00	14	00
Bessie Johnstoun	00	12	00
Jean Frizell	01	00	00
GALAWAY.—Margaret Stitt	00	14	00
AIR.—Janet Sloan	01	00	00
Janet M'Gines	01	00	00
Isobell Lambrughtoun	00	12	00
Barranfrew.—Isobel Anderson	01	00	00
Janet Stinstoun	02	00	00
CLYDSDALE.—Katrine Henderson	01	00	00
Margaret Douglas and Elspith Scott	01	10	00
Bessie Liper	00	14	00
Alexander Sime	02	00	00
John Hill	00	12	00
Elspith Jackson	00	14	00
Agnes Mair	01	00	00

Sumd. 20 06 00

Colectione destribute to the poor at Craford John, May 27, 1707.

Delivered to John Muir for the buriall of Isobell Carnduff in Evandalle	06	00	00
to Jo: Knox for Janet Scot and Janet M'Kinies	02	00	00
Item, Isobell Lamerochtoun and Janet Paton	02	00	00
to Andrew Corbet for Jo: Harron	01	10	00
Item, for Marion Leet and Jean Frizell	03	00	00
to the poor in the parish of Craford John	01	10	00
to Ja: Broun for Blench Johnstoun and Janet Ferguson	02	00	00
Item, for tuo poor in Haddom	01	10	00

Item, for Blench Ferguson	oo	14	o6
to Andrew Corbet for Marion Johnstoun	o1	oo	oo
to Mr. Stewart for the poor in Balmagie	o2	oo	oo
Item, for the poor in Gallaway	o3	oo	oo
to Ro: Maxwell for Alexander Syme and Elizabeth Jackson	o2	10	oo
to Jo: Davison for three wemen	o3	oo	oo
to Ja: Broun for Jo: Haladay	o1	oo	oo
to Jo: Watson for Janet Stinstoun	o1	oo	oo
to Ro: Fullertoun for Bessie Liper	oo	14	o6
to Frances Grame for Margaret Mitshall	oo	12	oo
Item, for Elspith Scot and her daughter	o1	10	oo
to Jo: Robson for Elizabeth Clove	oo	o7	oo
to Ro: Hamilton for a poor man	oo	14	o6
to Ja: Umpherstoun for tuo poor in Edenburgh	o2	oo	oo
to William Aiken for Agnes Mair	o1	oo	oo

Sumd	40	12	6

Collection destribute to the poor at Craford John, Agust 6 1707.

to James Currie for the poor in Lothian	o6	oo	oo
William Suanstoun for three poor in Tiviodalle	o2	oo	oo
James Scote for 4 poor in Anandall	o2	o8	o
John Glover for 7 poor in Nithsdalle	o4	12	o
Thomas Charters for 4 poor in Galaway	o2	11	o6
Hew Dickie for 5 poor in Air	o3	oo	o2
Andrew Wattson for 2 poor in Baranfrew	o3	oo	oo
Frances Grahame for 8 poor in Clydsdall	o6	oo	oo
Georg Jackson for 5 poor in Clydsdall and Baranfrew	o4	o4	o
Robert Grieve for 4 poor in Eskdall	o4	o3	o6
John Cuthell to John Girven	oo	12	oo
Mr. Stewart for the poor in Balmagie	o6		

Colection destribute at Craford John, for the use of the poor, February 9, 1708.

ANANDALL.—Ja. Mundall for Janet Fergusons funerall	o3	oo	oo
Ja. Mundall for Blench Johnstoun	o1	o4	oo
Ja. Mundall for Jean Johnstoun	oo	12	oo
Ja. Mundall for Janet Brynan	o1	oo	oo
Ja. Mundall for Bessie Johnstoun	oo	14	oo
To William Whyte for the poor in the parish of Craford John	o1	10	oo
GALAWAY.—William Stewart for Elizabeth Gurlay	o1	oo	oo
William Stewart for Margaret Stit	o1	oo	oo
TIVOTDAL.—William Suanstoun for Hellen Fish	oo	19	oo
William Suanstoun for Mary Nicoll	oo	19	oo

ESKDALL.—Jo: Grieve for Christin Scot . 01 00 00

GALLAWAY.—Jo: Bryce for Marion Mac-
burnie 00 14 00

NITH.—Ja: Mundall for Jean Nicolson . . 00 10 00

AIR.—Hew Dickie for tuo poor . . . 01 16 00

Destribute in Clydsdall and Baranfrew, February last, Thursday, 1708.

Margaret Summerall	01	00	00
Agnes Maer	00	12	00
Elspith Scot and her daughter . . .	01	04	00
Isobell Thomson	00	12	00
Ja: Forest	01	00	00
Bessie Liper	00	12	00
Rebekah Baillie	00	12	00
Elspith Cuming	00	14	00
Isobell Cosh	01	00	0
Alexander Thomson	00	14	00
Katrine M'Keltyre	00	14	00
Alexandet Syme	00	12	00
Elspith Jackson	00	10	00
a widow woman of Nistoun parish . .	00	12	00
	10	08	00

Destribbute for the usse of the poor at Craford John, May 3, 1708.

CLYDSDALL.—William Pillans for Margaret
Sumerall 01 10 00

NITH.—Harbert Walls for John Harron . . 02 00 00

Harbert Walls for Sarah Bell . . . 02 00 00

to William Whitte for the poor in the parish
of Craford John 01 00 02

Nether Ward of Clydsdall, Apryll 1708;
destribute to the poor.

Alexander Park	02	00	00
Alexander Sime	01	10	00
Janet Stinstoun	02	00	00
Katrine Mackelltyre	01	00	00
Elspith Jackson	02	00	00
Elspith Robison	02	00	00
Isobell Cosh	04	00	00
James Hamilton	03	00	00
Elspith Cuming	02	00	00
Elizabeth Yeuine	03	00	00
Received the recepts . .	22	10	0

Destribute for the usse of the poor at Craford John, Apryll 3, 1708.

Imprimis, to the poor of Craford John . . 001 10 00

Item, to the poor in Gallaway	.	.	02	08	00
Item, to the poor in Nithsdale	.	.	06	00	00
Item, to the poor in Baranthrow	.	.	04	00	00
Item, to the poor in Air.	.	.	02	03	06
Item, to the poor in Clydsdale	.	.	06	00	00
Item, to the poor in Eskdall and Forrest	.	02	18	00
Item, to the poor of Anandale	.	.	03	00	00
Item, to the poor of Stirling	.	.	03	00	00

Received the forsaid recepts . 30 09 06

Destribute for the usse of the poor, Craford John, November 15, 1708.

NITHSDALLE.—To John Harron	.	02	00	00
Bessie Johnstoun	.	01	00	00
Marion Sanders	.	02	00	00
Helen M'Millan	.	00	13	00
Agnes Glencors	.	00	12	00
ANANDALE.—Blench Johnstoun	.	01	10	00
Sarah Bell	.	01	00	00
CLYDSDALE.—To Bessie Aiken	.	00	14	00
Katrine Henderson	.	00	14	00
Christian Morrison	.	01	00	00
Agnes Mair	.	01	00	00
Elspith Cumin	.	01	00	00
Isobell Cosh	.	01	10	00
Marion Forrest	.	002	10	00
Ja: Martine	.	02	00	00
Elspeth Scot	.	00	12	00
Margaret Douglas	.	00	12	00
DUMBARTON.—Bessie Ewine	.	01	10	00
Elizabath Ewine	.	01	10	00
Alexander Simm	.	01	10	00
Jean Stinson	.	01	10	00
AIR.—Janet Weight	.	02	00	00

The Recepts from Nith. and Anan. 28 07 00

Destribute for the use of the poor in the Generall Meetting at Craford John, Janwary 17, 1709.

To John Herron	.	01	10	00
Marion Sanders	.	01	04	00
Sarah Bell	.	00	12	00
Blench Ferguson	.	00	12	00
Marrion Forrest	.	01	10	00
Agnes Mair	.	00	10	00
Margret Douglas	.	00	12	00
to the poor in Craford John	.	01	10	00

Received the forsaid recepts . 08 00 00

Destribute for the use of the poor at Craford John, May 3ᵈ, 1709.

to the poor in the paroch of Craford John .	oo	15	o6
depursed by William Swanstoun for the poor in Eskdall	o3	oo	oo
delivered to James Currie for the usse of severall poor	o8	oo	oo
to James Muir for Janet Scot . . .	o1	oo	oo
to Marrion Forest	o1	oo	oo

Received the forsaid recepts— Sumd 13 15 o6

Destribut for the use of the poor at Craford John, July 26, 1709.

ANANDALLE.—Sarah Bell	o1	oo	oo
Margrat Blekly	oo	12	oo
NITHSDALE.—Jo : Harron	o1	o4	oo
Marion Saders	o1	o4	oo
Marion Johnstoun	o1	oo	oo
Bessie Johnstoun	oo	18	oo
Marrion Teet	oo	12	oo
Jean Bell	oo	10	oo
Agnes Glencors	oo	o8	oo
GALAWAY.—Elspith Gurlay . . .	o1	10	oo
Marrion M'Burnie . . .	oo	10	oo
Margrat Stit	oo	10	oo
Elizabath M'Clore	oo	10	oo
AIR.—Janet Paton	oo	10	oo
Isobell Lamburghtoun . . .	oo	14	oo
BARANFREW.—John Park	o1	o4	oo
Isobell Anderson	oo	18	oo
CLYDSDALE.—Janet Scot . . .	o2	oo	oo
Marrion Forrest	o1	16	oo
James Martine	o1	10	oo
Alexander Simm	o1	o4	oo
Elspeth Jackson	oo	18	oo
Isobell Forrest	o1	o4	oo
Elspith Cummine	oo	18	oo
	14	o4	oo

Destribut to the poor at Hinshilwood in the paroch of Carnwath in Clydsdale, August first, 1709.

Bessie Aiken	o1	oo	oo
Margrat Douglas	oo	12	oo
Agnes Maer	o1	oo	oo
Rebekah Bailie	o1	oo	oo
Alexander Scouler	o2	oo	oo
James Hamilton	o1	oo	oo
to the poor in Carnwath . .	oo	16	o8
	o7	8	8

Craford John, November 3ᵈ, 1709. Destribute to the poor in
Nithsdalle.

Marion Sanert	02	00	00
John Harron	02	00	00
Marion Johnstoun	00	12	00
ANANDALE.—Sarah Bell	01	00	00
GALLAWAY.—Elspith Gurlay	01	00	00
Elisabath M'Clore	00	06	00
Margrat Stit	00	18	00
BARANFREW.—Jo: Park and Isobell Anderson	01	10	00
TIVOTDALLE.—Margrat Fish	00	14	00
CLYDSDALE.—Janet Scot	01	10	00
Isobell Hastie	01	10	00
BORROUSTOUNESS.—To a poor woman	01	00	00
AIR.—For the poor	00	16	00

Destribute to the poor at Craford John, February 28, 1710.

John Sheden	01	10	00
Janet Scot	02	00	00
Isobell Hastie	01	00	00
Elspith Gurlay	00	12	00
Elizabath M'Clore	00	12	00
Ja: Ferguson	01	10	00
Marrion Forrest	01	04	00
Alexander Syme	01	04	00
James Martine	01	04	00
Isobell Lameruchtoun	01	04	00
Thomas Craig	04	00	00

Destribut to the poor at Craford John, May 9, 1710.

CLYD.—Rebekah Baillie	00	08	00
Janet Scot	01	00	00
Marrion Forrest	00	12	00
Bessie Aieken	00	12	00
Ja: Martin	00	12	00
Jo: Shedden	00	12	00
Agnes Maer	00	12	00
STIRLIN.—Ja: Ferguson	00	12	00
GALL.—Elizabath Gurlay	00	12	00
Elizabath M'Clore	00	08	00
NITH.—For the use of their poor	04	06	00
For the poor in Craford John	00	13	00
BARRANFREW.—Alexander Sime	00	12	00
AIR.—Isobell Lamerughtoun	00	09	00

Destribute to the poor at Craford John, Jully 17, 1710.

AIR.—Isobell Lameruchtoun and Janet Gamell	03	10	00
Janet Paton	00	12	00
Thomas Hood	01	00	00

NITHSDALE.—Jo: M'Call for a poor woman	01	00	00
Ja: Mundall for the rest of the poor	06	02	00
TIVOTDALE.—Margrat Fish	01	00	00
Jo: Johnstoun	01	00	00
Mary Nicoll	01	00	00
ANANDALE.—Sara Bell	00	12	00
Margret Bleaklaw	00	08	00
GALL.—Mr. Stewart for their poor	01	10	00
CLYD.—Ja: Muir for the use of their poor	07	00	00
BARRANFREW.—Jo: Wattson for their poor	01	10	00
STIRLIN.—Ja: Ferguson	01	00	00

Distribution of the poors collections at Crawfoord John, October 24, 1710.

LINLITHGOW.—To Agnes Tod	01	00	00
For the poor in Air	01	12	00
CLYDSDALE.—To Alexander Sim	01	00	00
To James Clarkson	02	00	00
To Marrion Forrest	01	04	00
To Jonet Scot	01	16	00
To Rebeckah Baily	00	10	00
To Isobel Hastie	01	00	00
To Isobel Forrest	01	16	00
To Baranthrew poor	02	00	00
To Nithsdale poor	09	00	00
To Stirling poor, viz. James Fergusson	01	04	00
To Galloway to a poor woman	00	12	00
To Tiviotdale poor	02	14	00
To a poor woman in Crawfoordjohn	00	06	00

At Crawfoord John, February 23, 1711.

For the poor of Nithsdale, delivered to James Harkness	03	00	00
For the poor of Galloway, given to Mr. Stuart	01	10	00
For the poor of Lothian	00	06	00
To Robert Rickerton	08	00	00

At Crawfoord John, May 22, 1711.

To Hugh Dickie for the poor of Air	01	10	00
To the poor of Tiviotdale	01	10	00
To the poor of Anandale and Nithsdale	06	08	00
To the poor of Galloway	02	08	00
To John Scot in West Calder	04	00	00
To Marrion Forrest	01	06	00
To the poor of Crawfoord John	00	10	00
To the poor of Clydsdale	04	16	00
To the poor of Stirling	01	00	00

At Crawfoordjohn, February 11, 1712.

To Tiviotdale poor	03	00	00

To Nithsdale poor	08	00	00
To Marrion Forrest	01	00	00
To Robert Patoun	01	12	00
To the poor of Air	02	00	00
To the poor of Galloway . . .	02	02	00
To Andrew Old	00	18	00

At Crawfoordjohn, May 27, 1712.

To a woman in Crawfoordjohn parish .	00	10	00
To the poor of Stirling	03	00	00
To John M'Call	00	10	00
To John Steil	01	00	00
To Isobel Forrest	02	10	00
To Isobel Hastie	01	00	00
For the poor of Netherward of Clydsdale	00	10	00
To a man in Crawfoordjohn . . .	01	10	00
To William Wilson	03	00	00
To Elizabeth Atkine	01	00	00
To Alexander Wilson	01	10	00
To Jonet Boyd	01	00	00
To the poor of Airshyre . . .	02	00	00
To the poor of Galloway . . .	03	00	00
To the poor of Nithsdale . . .	03	00	00
To James Lang	01	00	00

At Thornhill, February 1713.

To the poor of Menteith . . .	12	10	08

At Kippoch, February 22, 1713.

To Elspith Cumming	01	10	00
To Elspith Robison	01	10	00
To Katharine M'kletyre . . .	01	10	00
To Thomas Hill	02	00	00
To Alexander Sim	02	00	00

At Crawfoordjohn, June 10, 1713.

To a particular person . . .	00	18	00
To Crawfoordjohn poor . . .	00	18	00
To the poor of Nithsdale . .	06	12	00
To James Dunlop	01	16	00
To the poor of Stirlingshyre . .	01	16	00
To the poor of Clydsdale . .	12	00	00
To the poor of Crawfoord parish .	01	16	00
To the poor of Greenock . .	01	16	00
To the poor of Linlithgow . .	03	10	00
To a certain poor woman . .	00	12	00
To the poor of Airshyre . .	03	12	00
To a certain poor man . . .	00	12	00
To the poor of Galloway . .	12	00	00

To	02	08	00
To the poor of Nithsdale (*sic*) . . .	02	08	00
To the poor of Clydsdale (*sic*) . . .	04	00	00
To a certain person	04	04	00

At Badshaw, September 27, 1713.

To a poor man at Arns	03	00	00
To poor folks in the place . . .	01	04	00
To a transient begger	00	02	00

At Pollock, October 5, 1713.

To poor folks in the place . . .	01	04	00
To Margaret Abercromie . . .	02	08	00
To John Mack	03	00	00
To a poor woman in Paisley . . .	01	04	00
To Elizabeth Keir	01	04	00
To Katharine M'Tyre . . .	02	00	00
To Isobel Rodger	02	00	00
To Elizabeth Jackson . . .	02	00	00
To Jean and Grizzel Patons . . .	04	00	00
To Elizabeth Cummin . . .	02	00	00
To John Malcom	02	00	00
To Elizabeth Robison . . .	02	00	00
To Jonet Paul	02	08	00
To Isobel Anderson . . .	02	08	00

At Dalry, October 10, 1713.

To poor folks in the place . . .	01	10	00

At Gaalston, October 19, 1713.

To John Mack's family . . .	02	04	00
To a begging man	00	06	00

At Crawfoordjohn, June 1, 1714.

To the poor of Linlithgowshyre . .	01	04	00
To the poor of Clydsdale . .	08	00	00
To the poor of Galloway . .	07	04	00
To W. M'F	15	00	00
To John Mack's wife . . .	01	10	00
The poor of Nithsdale . . .	10	00	00
To the poor of Greenock . .	01	10	00
To the poor of Stirlingshyre . .	03	04	00
To the poor of Crawfoordjohn parish .	01	08	00

At Crawfoordjohn, July 20, 1714.

To the poor of Nithsdale, with the allowance of the next Lords Days collection .	02	00	00
To Anandale poor the next collection at Coldoons			
To the poor of Merse	01	00	00

To the poor of Stirlingshyre 03 00 00
To Galloway poor 04 06 00
To John Macks wife 01 10 00
To the shyre of Air poor 04 00 00
To James Forrest 01 10 00
To Lishmahego poor 01 12 00
To Carrick poor 01 12 00
To Crawfoordjohn poor 00 17 00

At Caldercrooks, July 26, 1714.

To Jean Waddel 03 00 00
To Agnes Mair 01 00 00
To Alexander Waddel 01 00 00
To Christian Miller 01 10 00
To Jonet Scot 01 10 00
To Arthur Allein 01 10 00
To Isobel Watson 01 10 00
To Margaret Logan 01 04 00
To John Bolloch 01 06 0
To Bessie Lennox 00 12 00
To a creeple woman 00 06 00
To Jonet Marshal 00 14 06

At Crawfoordjohn, October 26.

To the poor of Galloway . . . 03 12 00
To an Irishman 10 00 00
To Isaack M'Millan 04 00 00
To Robert Fulton 07 06 00

At Caldercrooks, July 25, 1715.

To Margaret Logan 01 04 00
To John Henderson 00 12 00
To John Russal 03 12 00
To Rebeka Baily 01 04 00
To two begging women 00 07 00
To Christan Miller 01 10 00
To . . . . . Allein 00 12 00
To Andrew Auld 01 04 00

At Castlehill, August 8, 1715.

To Rebeka Baily 01 10 00
To Robert Aiton 01 00 00
To Jean M'Gahan 00 14 00
To Isobel Weir 01 16 00
To Bessie Aitken 00 12 00

At Crawfoordjohn, February 1716.

To Isobel Hastie 01 00 00

	£	s.	d.
To Elspith Jackson	01	10	00
To Isobel Anderson	01	04	00
To Agnes Patoun	01	04	00
To Margaret Abercrombie . . .	01	10	00
To John Malcom	01	04	00

At Crawfoordjohn, July 23ᵈ, 1716.

	£	s.	d.
To John Mack's wife	02	00	00
To the poor of Clydsdale . . .	02	00	00
To the poor of Nithsdale . . .	01	16	00
To the poor of Airshyre . . .	01	10	00
To Mary Gordon in Galloway . .	03	00	00
To Bessie Johnston at Minnyve . .	00	18	00
To the poor at Crawfoordjohn . .	00	10	00

At Crawfoord John, May 27, 1717.
[Nothing entered here.]

At Douglass, February 17, 1729.

Given to the poor by James Pawl, 40sh. which with the other collections was there distribute, viz.

Imprimis, to Thomas Henderson in Echelfechan	12	12	0
To Nithsdale	6	00	0
To Galloway	3	00	0
To Nether Ward	6	00	0
To Eskdale	3	00	0
To Agnes Inglis	3	00	0
To Annandale	1	17	0
To Margaret Ladlaw	0	12	0

At Braehead, February 3, 1740.

Given to the poor among the Community by James Paul the sum of 7 lit. sterling which was destribute among the said poor by the Rev. Mr. Jo: M'Millan and the General Meeting and came very seasonably being a time of dearth and scarcity by reason of the then storm.

At Crawfoord John, May 28, 1741.

Given to the poor among the Community by the said James Paul the sum of 10 lit. sterling of which was also distribute among the said poor by the Rev. Mr. Jo: M'Millan and the General Meeting and likewise came most seasonably being a time of great scarcity and dearth occasioned by the cold stormy season and great drought.

Given by James Paul for the use of the poor among the Community at different times.

	£	s.	d.
February 1729 (*sic*)	2	0	0
February 1740	7	0	0

	£	S.	D.
November 1740	10	0	0
May 1741	10	16	0

Received at the Communion at Auchensauch hill, July 23, 24, 26, 27, 28 and 29 days, 1712, of collection for the poor about 160 lib. 00ˢ. 00ᵈ.

	£	S.	D.
Whereof was given to the poor about the place	06	00	00
To a poor man in Craufordjohn . . .	01	04	00
Item, to	18	00	00
Item, to William Wilson	03	00	00
Item, to Isobel Hastie	03	00	00
Item, to Isobel Forrest	01	10	00
Item, to Robert Pinkerton	01	10	00
Item, to Margaret Calderhead . . .	01	10	00
Item, to Elizabeth Newlands . . .	01	00	00
Item, to Mary Gilkerson and Isobel Bar .	02	00	00
Item, to Andrew Black	01	10	00
Item, to Helen Cranston	01	00	00
Item, to John Scot	02	00	00
Item, to John Shedden and Rebeckah Bailie .	04	00	00
Item, to the poor of Nithsdale . . .	06	00	0
Item, to David Selkirk	03	00	0
Item, to Elizabeth Cummine . . .	01	16	0
Item, to Galloway poor	06	00	0
Item, to Agnes Mair	02	00	0
Item, to Stirline poor	08	08	0
Item, to Jean Paton	01	04	0
Item, to Andrew Old	02	00	0
Item, to Douglas fellowship . . .	02	00	0
Item, for Elizabeth M'Cloor . . .	01	00	0
Item, to Isaack M'Millan . . .	04	00	0
Item, to Nithsdale poor	08	00	0
Item, to Christian Brown . . .	01	00	0
Item, to Alexander Sim	01	10	0
Item, to Elizabeth Jackson . . .	01	10	0
Item, to Isobel Anderson . . .	01	04	0
Item, to Bessie Akine	01	04	0
Item, to criple wifes	00	19	0
Item, to a poor man	00	04	0
Item, to Tod	02	00	0
Item, to the poor of Air	07	04	0
Item, to Kathrine M'tyre . . .	01	00	0
Item, to Elizabeth Robison . . .	01	00	0
Item, to Burrestouness	03	00	0
Item, to Margaret Smelie . . .	01	04	0
	105	17	0

At Crawford John, July 29, 1712.

	£	S.	D.
Item, to	06	00	0
Item, to Jo: Ma L (?)	04	00	0
Item, to	02	10	0
Item, to	01	00	0
Item,	01	01	0
Item,	01	00	0
	01	05	0

[These last few entries are scribbled in.]

FINIS.

LORIMER AND CHALMERS, PRINTERS, EDINBURGH.

Marion, aged 8; John, aged 6; Frances, aged 4;
Kaitheren, aged 2.

John M'Millan in the paroch of Kirkmahoe :—Sarah, aged
4; Ann, aged 2.

John Edgar in the paroch of Tinwald :—Thomas, aged 16;
Sarah, aged 14; Hellen, aged 2.

Herbert Wells in the paroch of Tinwald :—James, aged 15;
Agnes, aged 6; Marion, aged 3.

Jean Bell in paroch of Tinwald:—Mary, aged 11; Sarah, aged 9.

William Edgar in the paroch of Tinwald :—Mary, aged 14;
John, aged 8; Jean, aged 1.

Adam Coldan in the paroch of Tinwald :—Agnes, aged 13;
Marion, aged 10.

John Blaak in the paroch of Tinwald :—William, aged 11,
Hellen, aged 8; Robert, aged 5; Marion, aged 3;
Elspith, aged 6 months.

Sarah Bell in the paroch of Tinwald :—John, aged 15;
Mary, aged 12; William, aged 6.

William Mathison in the paroch of Gretney :—Grizell, aged
6; John, aged 4; Janet, aged 2.

John Miller in Dryf, ansuered for himself, aged 16.

At Johnstoun, in the paroch of Calder, March 5, 1707.—

James Biggart, in the paroch of Eastwood :—James, aged
5 quarters.

John Selkirk, in the paroch of Old Munkland :—Agnes,
aged 12 hours.

John Miller in the paroch of New Munkland :—Joseph, aged
11 dayes.

Thomas Scot in the Barony of Glasgow :—William, aged 16;
Kaitheren, aged 9; John, aged 9 quarters.

Alexander Thomson in the Barony of Glasgow :—Margaret,
aged 16; Gabriell, aged 13; Marion, aged 10; William,
aged 8; Kaitherin, aged 5; Mary, aged 1.

Robert Urie at the Brige end of Glasgow :—James, aged
3 quarters.

Alexander Gillies in the toun of Glasgow, brother to Isobell,
aged 14; George, aged 10; James, aged 4.

At Sydehills in the paroch of Kilmacolm (undated).—

Robert Logan in the paroch of Kilmarinock :—William,
aged 14.

Alexander Yeuine in the paroch of Banill :—Janet, aged
20 weeks.

John Park in the paroch of Grinock :—James, aged 12;
John, aged 9; Marion, aged 4.

Robert Garner in the paroch of Kilmacolm :—James, aged
16 and 6 months; Jean, aged 14; Robert, aged 12;
John, aged 7; Alexander, aged 4.

At Kersland in the paroch of Dalray, March 16, 1707.—

John Walker in the paroch of Calder :—John, aged 12.

Margaret Urie in the paroch of Kilbryd :—Robert, aged 11 ; David, aged 6 quarters.

George Young in the paroch of Finick :—James, aged 7 ; Robert, aged 4.

Janet Stinstoun in the paroch of Nilstoun :—James, aged 4 ; Janet, aged 2 and 6 months.

Mathew Flager in the paroch of Cragie :—Elizabeth, aged 10.

At Plilanheed in the paroch of Evandale, March 18, 1707.—

John Mack in the paroch of Strathaven :—John, aged on year.

At the Haughead, Jun 6, 1707.—

John Davidsons child, Thomas, aged 6 weeks.

At Borroustouness, July 15, 1707.—

William M'Vays child, Ann, aged 3 quarters.

Tambandbill in Kilmadock, July 27, 1707.—

Janet M'Alester in Bonill parish :—William, aged 14 and half; Isobell, aged 11 ; Ann, aged 9 ; Margaret, aged 6 and half; John, aged 4.

John Paterson in Kinkaren parish :—Marion, aged 7 dayes.

James Smiths child, Helen, aged 9 weeks.

Johnstoun in Calder, Agust 1st, 1707.—

William Miller in Newmunkland :—Agnes, aged a moneth.

Suffield moor in Lasmehagow, Agust 3rd, 1707.—

David Young, New Munkland :—Marion, aged 12 weeks.

William Pillans in Torphichan :—John, aged 9 weeks.

Alexander Garner in Shots :—Mathew, aged 22 weeks.

James Russell, New Munkland :—James, aged 8 weeks.

John Marshall in Shotts :—Joseph, aged 20 weeks.

William Martine in Shots :—Janet, aged 25 dayes.

Marion Russell in Shots :—Alexander, aged 14 years.

Cora Miln in Lasmehagow, Agust 4, 1707.—

John Jeamisons children :—(Andrew Paull in Eastwood, parish, sponsor), Alexander, aged 16 ; John, aged 6 moneths.

West Brigtoun in Douglas, Agust 5, 1707.—

William Bradefoot in Douglas :—George, aged 9 weeks.

James Peetts in Douglas :—Thomas, aged 20 dayes.

Robert Kenady in Douglas :—James, aged 5 weeks.

John Stinstoun in Carmichall :—John, aged 8 dayes.

At Morisons Haven, December 23, 1707.—

Abel Heriots children :—Cristin, aged   , who was born Apryll 16, 1690; the second upon the 2nd November, 1694 ; the 3rd upon the 4 Jun 1696.

Williams Haals :—the eldest is 13 years, the 2nd, 9, the 3rd, three years.

In Kinnocher paroch (undated).

William Nicolsons children :—Elizabeth, aged 14 ; Mary, aged 12 ; James, aged 8 ; Ann, aged 8 ; Janet, aged 4.

Eodem die, in St. Andrews.—

> David Mathisons children :—Jean, aged 15 ; Andrew, aged 12 ; Christin, aged 9.

At Holstone, September 4, 1707.—

> James Umpherston and Marion Broun in Pentland wer married by the Rev. Mr. Jo. M'Millan. Their daughter, Anaple Umpherston, born July 29, 1708, was baptised at Pentland, August 4, 1708, by Rev. Mr. Jo. M'Millan.

1708, February 5.—

> Jo. Carsans child, in the parish of Glencarn, John, aged 6 moneths.

Feb. 8, att Craford John.—

> William Symintouns child, in the paroch of Lasmehagow, James, aged 6 moneths.

At Castellhill in the paroch of Lanerick, February 12.—

> Ja. Clarkson child, in the paroch of Carnwath, Michaell, aged 6 moneths.
> Jo. Reid in the paroch of Bothwell, John, aged 3 quarters.

At Blairmokhill in paroch of Shots, March 7, 1708.—

> Ro. Pinkertoun in Shots :—Agnes, aged 7 weeks.
> Andrew Aull in paroch of Munkland :—Robert, aged 20 weeks.
> James Main in paroch of St. Lauranc :—James, aged 15 weeks.

At Todhill in Old Munkland, March 21, 1708.—

> Jo. Jeamisons children, in the paroch of Eastwood (Andrew Paull, sponsor) :—Andrew, aged 10 ; Mary, aged 8.
> Will. Robison in the paroch of Bothwell :—John, aged 6 moneths.

Craford John, Agust 2nd, 1708.—

> Grizell Johnstoun in Crafordmoor :—Joseph, aged 4 moneths.

Carnwathmoor, Agust 8, 1708.—

> Jo. Hastie in paroch of Shots :—Beteritch [Beatrice], aged 18 weeks.
> Alex. Broun in paroch of Livistoun :—Janet, aged 8 dayes.
> Will. Broun in paroch of Carnwath :—William, aged 18 weeks.
> John Mann in paroch of Carnwath :—John, aged 19 weeks.
> Alex. Mathison in paroch of Carron :—Margaret, aged 16 weeks.
> Isobell Weir in paroch of Lasmehagow :—Isobell, aged an quarter.

Cader Crook, Agust 10, 1708.—

> Ja. Nisbet in paroch of Shots :—James, aged a moneth.
> Ja. Craford in New Munkland :—Robert, aged a moneth.
> Robert Steill in paroch of Shots :—Agnes, aged 8 weeks.

In the paroch of Killirion, Agust 22, 1708.—

> James Galbrath in the paroch of Kilmarinoch :—Jean, aged a quarter.

Craford John, Janwary 16, 1709.—
  Joseph Stotart in paroch of Douglas :—Marrion, aged 8 weeks.
  John Laurie in paroch of Carmichaell :—John, aged 12 weeks.
Castellhill in paroch of Lanerick, Janwary 23, 1709.—
  Thomas Barry in paroch of Carstairs :—Thomas, aged 10 weeks.
  John White in Carstairs :—Janet, aged 9 weeks.
  William Symintoun in Lasmehagow paroch :—Andrew, aged 6 weeks.
  Margaret Meikell in Lasmehagow :—Mary, aged 7 weeks.
  Isobell Forrest in paroch of Cambusnethen :—Elizabath, aged 14 weeks.
  Ritchard Dobbie in paroch of Carluke :—Thomas, aged 11 weeks.
Carphin Byars in paroch of Bothwell, Janwary 26, 1709.—
  Ja. Smith in paroch of Bothwell :—Walter, aged 3 quarters.
  Alex. Smith in paroch of Bothwell :—William, aged 3 quarters.
  Jo. Reid in paroch of Bothwell :—James, aged 10 weeks.
  Adam Selchrig in Old Munkland :—Isobell, aged an quarter of a year.
Craford John, July 24, 1709.—
  James Firth in paroch of Carmichall :—John, aged 11 weeks.
Serjan Law in paroch of Carnwath.—
  Jo. Haddock in paroch of Carnwath :—Robert, aged 15 weeks.
  Samuell Johnstoun in East Calder :—Elizabath, aged 9 weeks.
  Jo. Sheedden in parish of Bothwell :—Claud, aged 14 weeks.
  Will. Meikell in parish of Bothwell :—Robert, aged 20 dayes.
  Jo. Pet in paroch of Hamiltoun :—Marrion, aged 14 weeks.
  Bethea Sherilaw in paroch of Dalserf :—Margaret, aged 20 weeks.
  Jo. Meikell in paroch of Glasford :—Marion, aged 26 weeks.
  Patrick Love in paroch of Kilmacolm :—Margaret, aged 8 moneths.
  Margaret M'Crie in paroch of Kilbryd :—Janet, aged an year and 20 dayes.
  Jo. Marshall in paroch of Shots :—Jannet, aged a quarter.
  Ritchard Newlands in paroch of Shots :—John, aged 5 moneths.
  Jo. Christie in paroch of Shots :—Mary, aged a moneth.
  Alexander Dick in paroch of Shots :—Jean, aged 5 weeks.
  Jo. Newlands in paroch of Shots :—James, aged 6 moneths.
Cadder Crooks, Agust 2, 1709.—
  Jo. Samond in New Munkland :—Margret, aged a quarter.
  Jo. Miller in New Munkland :—Laudwick, aged half a year.
  Ja. Mitshall in Easter Kilpatrick :—James, aged a moneth.
  Hugh Miller in Old Munkland :—Robert, aged 26 weeks.